Angelos Michalopoulos

LIVING A SORROW AWAY FROM HAPPINESS

Translation:
Angelos Michalopoulos, Andreas Machairas

ATHENS 2015

© Angelos Michalopoulos, 2015.
This publication (work, material, book) may not be reproduced, transmitted or copied in part or in whole, by any means and in any form, nor may it be translated, adapted, adjusted, converted, or otherwise circulated or communicated to the public in any way or by any means, in accordance with the provisions of L. 2121/1993 and the Berne Convention for the Protection of Literary and Artistic Works, without the prior written approval of the author.
The reproduction of the typesetting and layout, the cover and the overall aesthetic appearance of this book by photocopying, electronic or any other methods for purposes of exploitation is strictly prohibited according to article 51 of L. 2121/1993.

www.angelosm.com
email: onelilo@angelosm.com

ISBN:978-618-81397-6-3

CHARACTERS:

Father

Mother

Their son Alexander

His wife Irene

Their daughter Nadia

Her husband Paris

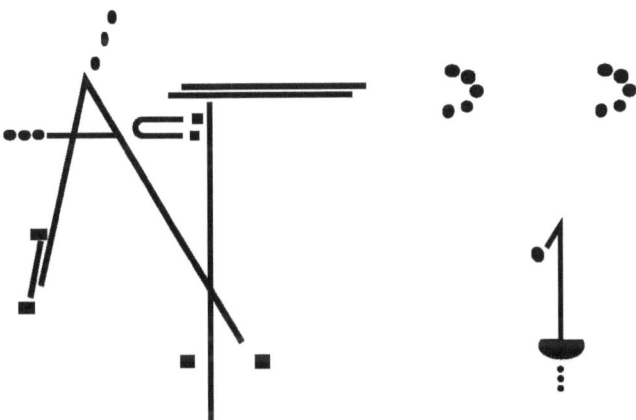

(*A three-bedroom apartment with a living room in the middle. Alexander and Irene are talking in their room*)

ALEXANDER (*Looking out the window while Irene is lying on the bed*): Ah, winter…The season my shortcomings like best. It's the time when the beautiful cowardice hidden in the wintry light feels an odd solidarity with any part of my life's backside that is still in love with the one dream which for so long I haven't been able to convince my normality to let me dream. The damn thing does everything it can to help my character flaws become less visible than during the summer because when it sheds its light on anything, it intends to hurt it first and then illuminate it.

IRENE: Why do I get the impression that you are referring to something that's more than just a simple winter?

ALEXANDER: You're right, I am. I'm talking about those different kinds of winter my loneliness leaves outside my door at night for me to choose one and put it in the next day's safe, so it can remind me during its course that sorrow doesn't perish when she meets a smile, she simply gets down on her knees and waits. Sitting in ambush, she waits for any insecurity of mine that might pass before her so she can seize her and make her confess which of my shortcomings still dare to be more ambitious than I am. She really wants to feel that she's not alone in her struggle to make me feel smaller, even more insignificant than what I already am, and so gain strength by confirming how much more optimistic than me my weaknesses are. Besides, these are the winters the first darkness will ask me to return a bit later after I drained all the pessimism out of them. It wants so much to get them back because it knows that there are many people who will soon be begging at its feet for them, hoping they might use them to unlock their own sorrow.

IRENE: Did you notice that when I walked into the room, out of all the expediencies at my disposal, I hung the biggest and most carnivorous one on the hanger behind the door?

ALEXANDER: Me too, as I walked in, I left the most innocent part of my logic on the table and, quickly overtaking the different words I intended to utter, started to fight with my ego about which one of us will be first to strong-arm my soul into giving me permission to attack you. I am ready to drill a hole in each of the thousand words I want to tell you, so they won't be able to convey to you the individual meaning I have imparted to each one of them. I want to make them not mean what they want to say, because I haven't been able yet to admit to myself how much I love the lie which just a little while ago, not knowing how to start hating it, I ended up worshiping.

IRENE: Please, if you have to worship something, worship your kindness. (*Pause*) By the way, how many '1s' fit in a '2'?

ALEXANDER: Less than what you hope for and more than what you can emotionally sustain. Don't forget that a couple is not comprised of just two people; it also includes their common sorrow and their common conscience.

IRENE: Why don't you include their common meanness too? Stop confusing a man's ego with the arrogance of his weaknesses. Arrogance is born of inadequacy, not strength.

ALEXANDER *(Turns and starts walking around the room)*: Are you trying to tell me that you believe in the existence of bulletproof bullets?

IRENE: I'm trying to tell you that there are hearts that don't care if they're struck by verbal bullets fired by the meanness of the people around them. They have so much pride in them that they know how to heal their injuries on their own.

ALEXANDER: Listening to you talk, I feel my malice dry faster than the blood that flowed out of the holes drilled by the words I fired at the skin of your soul. You know, this happens to me every time when, after having carefully and deliberately ripped thousands of holes in the nets of my self-awareness, I cast them into the deepest abysses inside me hoping to catch whatever I fear to realize. Unfortunately, most times I end up proving to myself that the most valuable part of my heart has more faith in you than it does in me. *(He grabs a magazine and starts leafing though it)*. Last night I couldn't sleep a wink and sat wide-awake for hours listening to that weird, incredibly piercing human sound which my loneliness lets out whenever I don't leave her alone…

IRENE: I think it's time I put back on the highest shelves of my mind the part of my logic I could never understand how it thinks.

ALEXANDER: And serve yourself the name of your next sorrow for breakfast?

IRENE: More likely serve myself to my next sorrow for breakfast.

ALEXANDER: Why don't you let me finish my own sentences for once? That way I might be able to realize what I'm trying to say!

IRENE: I don't let you finish your own sentences hoping I might realize what you are trying to hide behind their ending.

ALEXANDER *(Approaches and lies down next to her)*: Listening to us talk I sometimes think that there are more than two egos living among us.

IRENE: Two people with three egos! I like that! Our poor marriage carries them in its baggage, anxiously trying to find a way to let them off at the next stop of our reality, because it can't stand living with them anymore. *(Pause)* I'm afraid that once again I accidentally locked my self-awareness in my mind's warehouse where I store those truths that I have disappointed in the past with my behavior, the ones my self-awareness knows how to hide on the highest shelves when I'm not looking so I can't easily reach them.

ALEXANDER: Make sure you're not present the next time you open it.

IRENE: I couldn't bear that! You know, I was always impressed by how few things fit in my truth.

ALEXANDER: Especially new truths.

IRENE: I was always astounded by how much roomier than my truth my ego is.

ALEXANDER: Egos are like that, they're so greedy, so insatiable! Take mine for example. Each time I thought it couldn't fit anything more in it, it managed to surprise me, challenging me to bring it more pieces of my life to swallow.

IRENE: You mean more truths to swallow.

ALEXANDER: More like happinesses. Why are you asking me, you know so much more about this than I do.

IRENE: I won't reply since the answer itself, a second after I utter it, will give birth to a cunning question, which I'm not sure I'm ready to look in the eyes right now.

ALEXANDER: Me either. I'm afraid that this damned question will force me to unhook my hope from the back of the only door my normality uses when she wants to lock me in myself, so I can't get out and meet the explanations I ask of my own potential.

IRENE: And perhaps along with them, the cheap excuses you keep on feeding your own future so that once again you can attempt to explain to it why you will fail to do what you promised it.

ALEXANDER: Perhaps.

IRENE: It's this question that once again will force me to end up, five minutes before the end of each hour, threatening the next one to go through it cursing its every second if it doesn't bring me what I have asked for. I can't live like that anymore. I already have enough problems trying to manage the different kinds of egos I have, which have been negotiating among themselves for hours trying to retain the privileges that I personally granted to each one of them separately. All of them want to avoid having to adjust to the new dimensions required of them by that version of myself that my self-confidence loves above all others. It's the one that, because it doesn't want to come near the others, has been patiently waiting for days now to introduce itself anew to me at the spot where my life's next steep uphill begins, the one which my arrogance has been desperately trying to convince me to climb since it fell in love with my future some time ago.

ALEXANDER *(Takes hold of her hand)*: There's something I've been meaning to tell you for some time now. I am never alone anymore, not even when I am on my own. Every time you are not near me, my sorrow comes and settles a few inches away from me and momentarily makes me feel a kind of invisible need, as if I am morally obliged, to keep her company, to take care of her. I feel that if I don't pay her any attention I am mistreating, almost disrespecting, an important part of myself.

IRENE: Please, don't let me carry around those overweight tears that hardly know how to cry anymore. I can no longer lift them. Face it. I am not ready to become your private storm's sole conversational partner, the only person that can understand its language and translate for you everything it no longer knows how to tell you. My soul, already holding the key, no longer knows how to open her doors to your magnificent rage, which is right outside banging furiously on them trying to break them down.

ALEXANDER: I don't know why, but today for some reason am reluctant to listen to what my lips want to tell me. I want to let my silence caress them until it manages to extract from them those words that contain solely the meaning of what she wants to say…

IRENE: I was always impressed by your facility in letting your silence evoke emotions in me which you could never elicit.

ALEXANDER: Don't interrupt me! Let me finish before I forget what I don't want to tell you. I want to let that word of mine that hides behind my silence free to caress any hesitation, any fear the rest of my body has been trying to hide from me for some time now. I am tired of trying, each time our meanness manages to get into our mouths ahead of us, to deform my heart until she takes on a shape that satisfies you, one you may even possibly like. I am tired of seeing her, while you are getting ready to open your mouth to say something, doing hundreds of multiplications and divisions, drenched in her own sweat, to be in time to put into my words all that I don't want anymore to say, all that you have so insistently asked her for already.

IRENE: How many calculations fit in a heart that has already seen the dawn of the next day defeat her owner?

ALEXANDER: How many fit in a dawn that has already beaten at arm wrestling the next sunset coming in a few hours? *(Pause; He gets up and moves back to facing the window)* You know, my laughter is no longer afraid of me.

IRENE: What do you mean?

ALEXANDER: I mean that I can no longer look into the eyes of my self-esteem, in which I have personally stored the most morally inaccessible highlights of my life, the ones I cannot traverse unless I take with me all the reserves of my dignity.

IRENE: I am disappointed that your laughter learned over time to think, I am annoyed that now it first looks to find a way not to embarrass you by laughing, before it finds a reason to let itself free to simply do what it was born for.

ALEXANDER: There are days when I feel that, having first donned that skintight courage of mine that believes more in my stupidity than in me, I must start attacking my future before I realize that my own hopes stopped hoping in me long ago.

IRENE *(Interrupting him):* Do you think that your stupidity is stronger than you?

ALEXANDER: I don't know. *(Pause)* Probably. So, after putting it on, I start walking for hours on the edge of my personal abyss trying not to tread on its most sensitive spots, the ones that already hurt it because it was never able to find a way to heal them. It's the abyss in which I am forced to cross rivers of an incredibly black liquid, rivers whose every drop is a sad moment of my life. I forge them for hours, immersing my entire body up to my neck, trying to satisfy my life's hard-bitten sergeant, my self-criticism, which is constantly on top of me, shouting slogans in favor of my cowardice and against any optimism I might still have left. At the end of my ordeal, my biggest sorrow is waiting to explain to me what she wants from me, what favor she expects from me today in order to agree to leave me alone with my serenity even for just a short while.

IRENE: What makes you believe that you know what to do when you are alone with your serenity?

ALEXANDER *(Does not respond)*

IRENE: Do you know how many times each week my past draws near me uninvited and asks me to thank it for all that it hasn't done to me yet?

ALEXANDER: I know, I know… I know those moments. I know very well what it's like to feel that the winters of your life have gathered together in the sharpest corner of your heart and just managed a minute ago to give birth to their worst day ever, which they want to immediately place in the middle of the happiest moment of your next day.

IRENE: These are the moments when you see from afar your heart's loneliness, her head bent, slowly advancing towards you, with a stride that wants to place each step a cowardice ahead of the last one and an optimism behind the next one, a stride that has already been defeated by its very own hopes. Once she is in front of you and lifts her head, you see a face that is vehemently cursing you. At first you have the impression that it looks like yours but, as time goes by, you realize that using magic tricks borrowed from your misery, she has managed in a very bizarre way to distort it to the point of making it seem like the face your rage would like you to have.

ALEXANDER: Looking at you, I feel as if my smile is drilling holes in its own body so that it won't be able to keep inside it all that I want it to carry for me to the front door of your soul.

IRENE: How can a person protect himself from the lightning bolts his own mind throws at his happiness?

ALEXANDER: By pretending he doesn't know in which part of his private sky the clouds live?

IRENE: By pretending he can't see the vomit just given to him as a gift by any question in his mind that refused to answer why he ended up loving it more than its answer.

ALEXANDER: It's a tough life for any person who is constantly in love with the questions he means to ask his future, almost ignoring the answers it leaves itself at the edge of his mind each morning for him to open and find in them part of the opinion the people that love him have of him.

IRENE: Sadly true…

ALEXANDER: It's so hard trying to walk among the fingerprints left by your honesty the last time she visited you without erasing a single one!

IRENE: I have the impression that you would do anything to avoid stepping on them, so you won't distort the man who will emerge out of who you became today to escape from who you were yesterday.

ALEXANDER: How the hell do you manage to access my feelings before I do?

IRENE: The same way you have managed to wedge a part of your soul in any phrase that's frantically trying to get out of my mouth before my middle-age logic can grab it by the neck and quickly transform it into a successful silence.

ALEXANDER: Hold on a second, take a break and come help me adapt the strength of my self-confidence to the freedom I have just given to the one question the infinity that lives in me has to ask me. That cunning devil rushes off to sneak ahead of me into any part of my misery I have left unguarded and then leave me waiting for hours, until it is ready to announce to me what my melancholy wants me to bring her today so she will leave me alone, even for a short time, at the end of the day.

IRENE: How will you manage that?

ALEXANDER: Pretending that I don't know how to ignore it.

IRENE: Why, don't you think you can play around for a while, catching each word you are ready to utter with your tongue and, by pushing it against the sides of your mouth, manage to get a better sense of its flavor, try to better understand what you are really trying to say?

ALEXANDER: Hell, why is the darkness that lives in my mouth smarter than all the others?

IRENE: You are really scared of it, aren't you?

ALEXANDER: Frankly, I really am. Why, aren't you? Which part of yourself do you think enjoys more making you suffer than this damned darkness that lives inside your mouth?

IRENE: Before I answer you I want to arm my face with a smile that still remembers how to lie. I am not sure which, maybe the one that is unable to realize, each time it's not looking, how much emotional trash I throw into it!

ALEXANDER: I think that the barrel of that gun that lives with its safety off in the middle of my mouth suddenly lost all the privileges my best delusions granted it long ago. I was always impressed by how easily you created fears in me out of materials which, every time they passed through the corridors of my soul to come meet me, pretended they didn't recognize each other. It's really impressive how much better you are becoming at this as you grow older. You are so good at convincing me that the time has come for me to start disentangling my mind from its most valuable questions, those questions that for years now have been wrapped around its weakest spot and, after doing that, at helping me untangle the second half of my life from the un-answered questions of the first one.

IRENE: Isn't this battle the daily Mount Everest each one of us is forced to climb while listening to thousands of fans of his melancholy cheering him on right and left, urging him to go on?

ALEXANDER *(Raising his hands up high)*: Listening to you makes me want to wrap myself around the only part of my soul that years ago decided to always stay motionless each time my life forces her, with the problems she keeps on dumping on her, to run fast in order to survive.

IRENE: It doesn't move because it can't or because it feels that by doing so it will betray the remainder of your soul?

ALEXANDER: I hope it's the latter. I want to start walking towards the opposite side of my head from where my most optimistic thought seeks to go, observing the end of it having already started renovating its own beginning.

IRENE: People are right when they say that if you don't get closer to the future your past has ordered for you, you will never learn how to find the end of the sadness that is caused by the fire your own mind lit to burn the dry weeds that grow unchecked in the middle of its most fertile section.

ALEXANDER: And where the greedy laughter hidden inside the most barren, unproductive part of your sorrow starts, the one that is anxiously waiting to see what kind of seeds you want to plant in its innards today. What makes you think, however, that I know in which spot of my mind this fire that gives birth to the embers of my every action ends?

IRENE: I wish I lived in a world where a fire, no matter how long it lasted, could never produce anything but ashes and embers!

ALEXANDER: Sorrows? Why don't you mention sorrows?

IRENE: I find something exquisite in that an ember's past is a fire that never sought to discover the reason it started, the reason it taught itself from an early age to take such pleasure in destroying whatever it touches.

ALEXANDER: I agree. A fire is born long before its first flame. Possibly even in a different spot from where its first flame is born.

IRENE: You mean to tell me that a tear's past is a sad soul that doesn't know why she is sad, has no idea why she gave birth to it?

ALEXANDER: It is often the past of the owner of the soul that gave birth to it. Did you know that by always looking backwards you frequently stumble upon a part of yourself that has been waiting for years to convince you that it never wanted to meet you in the first place?

IRENE: Perhaps, perhaps...

ALEXANDER: Does your silence want to talk to me without you being present? Do you, perhaps, want to confide in me a new kind of truth, which not even you know how to entrust to words which you are certain will be able to convey the meaning of what you wish to express without keeping the most important part to themselves?

IRENE: Will you please let me grab my truth by the waist and convince her to even briefly touch the most sensitive part of your silence?

ALEXANDER: You mean the only part of it that wants to persuade my mouth to tell all?

IRENE: No, I mean exactly what I said.

(Alexander places his left hand in front of his mouth, takes out a silence from inside him and, unfolding it very tenderly, takes two steps forward and gently lays it in the middle of her palm)

ALEXANDER: You know, I am beginning to think that I belong to the questions of my silence.

IRENE: Maybe you belong to her ambitions too.

ALEXANDER: You may be right... I always believed that silence is those truths that, because man knows how invaluable they are, he ends up keeping forever locked inside him.

(On the couch located in the middle of the living room sits Nadia. The door opens and in comes Paris back from work, sweaty, exhausted, with a briefcase in hand, which he drops on a chair and then sits down on the couch)

PARIS: What a day, what a day! Who the hell told them that I can daily face what I lived through today? How much longer do they think I can take this? How much longer will I be able to look at my dignity in the mirror every morning, push it a little to the right and a bit to the left until it fits the boundaries of the personality everybody around me expects me to have and wearing next to my skin all the mistakes I made yesterday, or rather the ones my shortcomings made on my behalf yesterday, to go out into reality so I can realize once more how much more resourceful than me they truly are? I wish I knew how to hide my next right decision from my mistakes. How to be in time to grab it from their dirty hands before they convince it to run away with them. I can't, I simply can't...I can't keep borrowing every day more and more of my future from those parts of my life which I am afraid to admit that the time has come to confess to the backside of my self-confidence that they are mine.
(With his right hand he grabs his tie and loosens it, then he changes his mind and tightens it again keeping his hand on the knot) What color will my favorite freefall have today? How many hermetically sealed doors of my dignity will I have to knock on today till I find the first one that will agree to step aside and let me through? I can no longer stand, every morning when I wake up, to anxiously rush, as fast as I can, to put on new masks on the mistakes I made yesterday, so that I won't be able to recognize them no matter how many times I bump into them today. How many of my insecurities can I leave at the same spot in every dawn that the sun intentionally leaves unlit, so they can help me find where I've put those magic tricks of mine with which I will try to entertain the time I want to devote to my sorrow today in order to convince it to not take each minute in its right hand and hit me on the head with it?

    I no longer know how to keep on talking to my future without saying anything to it. By god, I just feel like grabbing my lips and tearing them off, not from my face but from their

true origin, my ego, and walk for hours holding them in my right palm, constantly staying at least a sorrow away from the path I would have followed if I were a happy man, a man who has the ability to understand what the slogans his misery is shouting from afar are trying to tell him. That way I could see what it's like to live without having constantly in my mouth the power of my worst word, the weakness of my worst self. My most exquisite ruins have become my sweat's most precious hopes, my sorrow has turned into my previous future, the heavy breathing of my thoughts into my next scream. How much different from who I am could I stand to become, I wonder, just so I could please those who pray I don't change anything on me? How many more post-midnight exhibitions of my cowardice can I fit into a night that is pleading to give me all its darkness because it fears it even more than I do?
(Nadia gets up from the couch and walks back and forth in front of him a few times, looking at him as if she just saw him for the first time in her life) I feel as if every word that lives in your gaze right now is looking me over as a potential buyer of a used car who doesn't believe what the salesman is telling him and is suspiciously glancing first at him and then at the car. Stop trying to lower my price. Don't forget you have already bought me years ago.

NADIA *(Sarcastically)*: Hello, beloved song of my distress! You are right. I did buy you but I didn't buy your misery. Every time I see you I feel as if your misery devised a brand new way for you to be miserable. At work today, did you manage once again to live through a day in which your unhappiness won more times than you did? Did you have to go through a day that had more sorrows than hours? Again?

PARIS: A lot more.

NADIA: How the hell do you manage every day to be better at being worse? Sometimes I see you standing huddled up against your loneliness and I wonder: if your adolescence could see you, would she recognize you? Face it. The only part of yourself that's still ambitious is your mediocrity. Every day she wants to improve, be the best she can be. You are a person who's sleepy even when you are sleeping. In love with the most middle path in your life, in love with that behavior of yours which demands to cut the average you endlessly use to produce every thought of yours into many pieces, to make sure that she will manage to get into the one which is closest to its absolute middle. It is this behavior that fights tooth and nail to keep you away from anything that is different, original, from any endeavor that demands of you to move away from what you are and take some risk, from every fight that might end up in something that doesn't resemble a convenient draw.

How can you keep refusing to realize that it's this same behavior that every morning, as soon as you get up, pushes you into the image your self-awareness sees when you turn your back on her to rush off, as fast as you can, before she has time to ask you her first question? It is this image of yourself that has already directed you before you get a chance to direct it. Everything calculated to the inch by the complete lack of imagination that always cares for your own good, because it knows better that anyone what suits you most, knows how few things you have to achieve in your life to convince yourself that you have succeeded. *(Shouting)* Not for me, though! This bizarre love of yours for the mediocre is choking me to death. To death, you hear?

Who did I marry? What did I marry? A black and white copy of the youthful hope you once had to become what you promise every morning now when you re-christen yourself "almost successful" to escape from the claws of your self-criticism, which, before you even get out of bed, rushes out of the room so it won't be forced to make eye contact with you. *(Raising her hands up high)* What self-awareness am I talking about? In your case, not even your stupidity takes a day off. You take her with you everywhere you go, to make sure that you always remain faithful to the person you do your best to not discover that you are.

PARIS: Can you please put a condom on your words? I can't bear listening to their echo piercing me as they attempt to locate all the spots in me where one of my most capable sorrows already drilled in the past, those that already hurt a lot and make them hurt even more.

NADIA: You are your stupidity's pimp, the man who prostitutes her on the sidewalks of your mind so he can pay the bills which the repeatedly failed orgasms of your mediocrity bring him one after the other at the end of each day. You are a man who writes by erasing, a man who prefers to permanently live in the basement of a life that is meant to be a high-rise. For ever in love with your previous light, the one you no longer want to know how to switch on so you won't have to learn how to switch it off, you have now reached the point where you detest anything shining you might see before you because it reminds you of the promises you made to yourself on that day in your teens that you were later forced to rip from your diary to avoid having to follow the advice of your self-awareness and toss the whole thing into the trash.

PARIS *(Exhausted, almost whispering)*: Listening to you talk, a second desert, even vaster, even stronger, more ambitious than my own, is insistently asking me to let it be born inside me right now.

NADIA *(Indifferently)*: Okay, whatever. In what part of your future did you bury your past so that you won't have to see it, you miserable man? Don't you know that every day you are condemned to compare yourself to the person you were yesterday? Don't you understand that every night we all have to sweep off the floor the very ruins we created during the day that just ended and put them to sleep next to our bed before we can go to sleep ourselves? Because we won't be able to sleep if they don't fall asleep first.

What desert are you talking about? Even the desert you mentioned, after living inside you for a while, will choose to self-exile in the pleasure felt by any of your mistakes, any of your defeats that knows it can become happier the further away it lives from you. By God, I've never seen a man lay concrete, as carefully as he can, over the seeds which every day he plants at the same time in the most fertile fields in his head, to make sure that tomorrow will not betray him by giving birth to something more ambitious, something more capable than what he can stand to be. Poor little man, you have become the bittersweet peddler of your cardboard clout, which was born to encompass anyone around you except yourself.

PARIS: Now I understand why they say that, when a person doesn't know what to feel, just so he can satisfy the fog that demands to be the one who will give birth on his behalf to the next minute of his life, he ends up attacking anything he finds in front of him.

NADIA: You are a peddler of an abused grandeur who is struggling to understand what each orgasm of his sorrow is trying to tell him at its climax. If you knew how to shed tears you wouldn't cry. If you knew what to understand, you wouldn't wonder endlessly around your questions. If you knew what to feel, you would be able to look your soul in the eyes without feeling that you should take a step back to avoid soiling her. If you knew how to take the next step forward you wouldn't sink in the very vomit of your most cowardly thought. You live every minute of your life lying down with your arms around your previous laziness and your next excuse. You live every minute watching your life not wanting to stop to take you with her, passing you by assuming she has nothing to gain by wasting time living with you.

PARIS: I don't know what pains me most. To admit that you are right or that you don't know what you are talking about? The only cheerful door my life has is located on its backside, where the plaster on the walls of my image is ready to peel off because I only have enough paint to maintain the front ones. It is there that every night I take out the huge garbage bags full of all my character traits that my self-criticism threw out that day, even though I know that later at night my various thoughts will, like the neighborhood cats, rush over to tear into them and find out what's inside them. I do my best to not step on them when I go out the next morning for a stroll on the sidewalk of the front side of my life and make a fool of myself to you, all of you.

My soul's pockets have in them many more draws than victories, more lazy whispers than well trained, bold words. You can't imagine how totally naked I feel each time the next victory of my life comes and stands before me, staring at me with those arrogant, incredibly intense, nearly white eyes, making my knees almost buckle. With a single blow it can throw me down, even lower than the apology I owe myself for all the things I did to it all these years each time I couldn't find the courage to say "no" to my most cowardly "yes" and "yes" to my most courageous "no".

NADIA: You can't imagine how much I enjoy seeing you spreading all the "nos" you have hidden inside you all over the breakfast table, unable to decide which ones you will take with you today to the office to help you represent your inability to say "yes", to simply agree.

PARIS: Every morning, as soon as my day's main gate opens up, I see my normality rush to raise my storefront shutters and start selling me at a discount. Right away I run like mad to prepare myself so that I'm in time to pass through my private miracle before it manages to ask me who I am, but I always find the door closed. Out of breath, I bang on it once, open it and start anxiously breathing in one by one, as deeply as I can, those breaths of my life that haven't realized that they are completely transparent, that I can easily see through them, the ones I can quickly tell that they don't want to give me the necessary oxygen, the optimism, the strength that I need to succeed.

I rush to help my day escape through the back door of my happiness, so later that evening she won't have a chance to see me set up from scratch the winners podium and then sit across from it, staring at it resting at the highest point of the day completely empty, with no emotion of mine wanting to go stand on it. I sit there until the fading light of the sunset denies me my right to see my cowardice climb this step and prepare itself to award the dreams it will soon give birth to on my behalf. When you live a blindingly empty, cowardly life, you no longer need anything to fill it up, you just let your own fears do it for you. Thus, at the end of each hour that goes by being madly in love with your ambiguity, you end up realizing that there is a part of you that has the ambition to be even emptier than you are, perhaps more empty than a perfect vacuum.

NADIA: Indeed. When a perfect vacuum is not empty enough for you…

PARIS: The next step of my life has been looking for days now for the spot within me where it left its keys, and I for the spot in my soul where my life hid her first aid kit. I need this step, I need it badly because, trying to go through the rainbow my most courageous hopes painted for me, I injured certain parts of my heart which I don't know how to heal because I no longer know how to feel. I want to grab from the sky the first horizon I find and carefully wrap it around my body, hoping it might be able to protect me with its splendor by shielding my truth from the attacks of the guilt that I myself give birth to in the minds of the people I love. My damn purity, each time she decides to illuminate me from the backside of my body, makes me watch on the wall of my alternate life the shadow of my body that contains more battle-ready questions than scared answers. This is the final payment of a lie that has decided to tell only truths from now on.

These are the rare moments when my life lets me dive into her summary to try to understand how I ended up becoming someone who, if I saw him before me when I was eighteen I would die of fright. I would like to gather as much speed as my heart can bear and run until I stretch my body enough to be able to dive into the unseen side of my courage hoping to discover all that I hid there long ago.

I am tired of constantly rushing to get to meet myself before my cowardice does, so that I will be able to open those dusty albums with my old photographs before they decide to self-immolate in front of my memory to avoid revealing to me who I once was. They are the ones that contain the photographic proof of a lost tomorrow, the proof of a tear that died because it won, a joy that didn't know how to lose the disillusioned breaths of an optimism that never dared to learn how to fight, because from an early age it was so good at hiding. I see in those pictures the gaze of a person whom the universal invisible chose, out of all people to live inside him, the gaze of a person who can stand to have a better relationship with his silence than with any of his words.

NADIA *(Sarcastically)*: To your health, oh great lover of your own failure! You hapless fool, not only didn't you become what you wanted, but you did not even dare to be who you were. Face it, not even your life's trash wants to belong to you anymore.

PARIS: Yes right, I did not even dare to be what I already was. *(Struggling to gather all the strength he has in him and push it to the front of his mouth so it can protect him from her attacks)* At least, I am not alone, I have my emotions, I have my soul which, though heavily indebted to any sorrow I've forced her to constantly live arm in arm with, continues to keep me company, making me feel wounded but human. Better than you, who lives the life of a person who, because you think you're so perfect, cannot remember how you were then, in the old days, when you resembled a human. Who are you anyway? You live a life breathing in with every breath of yours the despair of your most magnificent solitude, the triumphs of your negativity, having forced every word of yours to take down the number "1" from the backside of your heart's door and install it on its own back, leaving very little space for any meaning you have given it to convey. You should know that there is no heavier burden in the world than this number "1" you love so much.

    Not even your loneliness wants to keep you company any more. What have you achieved in your life beyond surviving by milking throughout every day the various trophies your beloved "1" has brought you? I am talking about the ones that it leaves at your feet, having first convinced them to dive into the minds of the people you oppress so that they'll show you a little more counterfeit respect, hoping you will be able to make your ego forget how miserable it is even for just a short while. You live alone among hundreds of lies that refuse to give you back, even for a minute, the piece of your logic you have forced each one to carry inside it on your behalf. How much can you possibly like the hypocrisy with which the same people who fear the meanness of your mediocrity even more than you do rush, as soon as they see you coming, to wrap themselves in the cardboard respect contained in the cheapest compliment they can find, to convince you that they don't despise you as much as you think?

NADIA: I cannot figure out how you manage to talk while you are eating out of the trash that your self-confidence left you the last time in your life you truly felt insignificant.

PARIS *(Does not reply)*

NADIA: What happened, can't you convince a single word of yours to come up to your mouth anymore?

PARIS: You know, silences sometimes conceal extremely effective Trojan horses in them. *(Explodes)* You have become my winter, a winter that is so proud of the pain he dishes out to the people around him, that he's come to believe that since he is the best season there is no reason for him to end. Every time you intend to meet someone, you take out the sharpest knife at your disposal, then cut off the edges of your soul that are more rotten than others and throw them at his face, while at the same time you disparagingly take out of her one by one and throw forcefully on the table all those emotions that you are unable to feel for him.

    You seem to really need to shatter into a thousand pieces any peacefulness, any joy you see around you, even that of the person you love, believing that by taking out the meanness from inside you and spreading it all around you, you will make the part that spawned it hurt less. I have never seen anybody else get so much pleasure from grabbing the dirtiest piece of trash he can find in him and, after wrapping it in the leftovers of his own mind, install in its center the most precious ornament of his soul and take it out to show it to the people he loves.

NADIA: I have never seen anybody celebrate every defeat of his so much! I won't sit here to be lectured on behavior by someone who lets the blackest darkness he meets during the night teach him how to clothe his soul in white for the coming day. Are you any different than a miserable tree that doesn't want to let its branches sprout a single leaf, a sign of life, any beautiful creation from within them? Are you any different than someone who trusts his shortcomings to protect him from anything his virtues want to achieve?

PARIS: Stop trying to explain to the noose that's been circling around my head for some time now the ending of its every dream, it never wanted to understand it in the first place.

NADIA: I have never seen anyone refuse to even listen to what the happiest moments in his life want to confide in him.

PARIS: They ask me to stand by them, to try to feel them until, after talking to them for a while, the password of every injury I have hidden inside them comes itself to deliver the numbers that open its door so I can get inside and hug it till it no longer needs be an injury, until it no longer needs to cause pain. *(Lowers his head)* Do you know how many parts of my soul no longer respect me?

NADIA: Let me tell you something. I am not your life's emergency exit. I am not the one who will rescue you when you throw yourself into the sea and the first thing you do is anxiously turn your head upwards to see who might be even slightly interested in saving you. Aren't you impressed by the fact that, every time this happens, the sole emotion of yours that is there, with life jacket in hand ready to throw it to you, is your sorrow?

PARIS: Talking to you I feel as if I forgot how to understand and remembered how to start questioning. I need to let out one of those screams that always had so much rage in them that at the end of each fight with myself they managed to transform themselves into endless serenities, screams that can no longer stand to be just screams, so they appear before me, four inches from my face, demanding that I teach them how to become infant melodies. I really want to help those whispers that never asked me why I didn't let them speak find the courage to start shouting, to wake me up from the lethargy inside where I was abandoned by the one silence I loved more than any word in my life.

NADIA: Are you sure that you entirely fit in what you just said?

PARIS: I no longer know how to balance on the northern side of my soul, the side that stays constantly dark, where the ice of my reality never melts because it doesn't know how to get rid of its frigidity, doesn't know how to leave behind it the coldness to which it has pledged eternal loyalty, doesn't know how to lead a life without being constantly locked up in that sorrow which for years has loved it more than any other.

NADIA: While we were talking, I felt your self-worth come out of your body, take two steps and then suddenly turn around and start spitting you in the face.

PARIS: I think the time has come for me to see you without the stage props my mind's second thoughts always set up trying to convince me to continue living with you, to convince me to help the logic your happiness prefers to apply in its attempt to save our marriage from those black clouds which tomorrow never stopped bringing us after each of our fights.

NADIA: Okay, okay. I strongly advise you to start distorting your thoughts, the first thoughts that come to your mind, until you stop thinking on behalf of your ego and start thinking on behalf of your happiness.

PARIS: And you should stop trying to distort our marriage to the point of making it seem like something that looks good on your resume, especially the part that concerns me. *(Pause)* I wish you knew how many times, for the sake of our happiness, I became that insecurity of mine which I hate more than all the others, just so I could carry on through and reach the end of each day without self- destructing!

NADIA: Enough, enough. It's eight already. The time has come when your day will ask you how many new character flaws you discovered you have today.

PARIS: I was always impressed by the fact that, while you have so painstakingly created the facade of your apparently limitless wellness, and while you rush up and down your battlements defending against the various barbarians of your reality who attack the walls of the castles to which you have assigned the task of shielding you from who you are, knowing you so well, I see a woman who, above all, is busy trying to convince her previous melancholy to not fall in love with her next joy. You know better than anyone how to defend against your external enemies and have become so good at building, faster than anyone I know, such high walls that hardly anyone will be able to defeat them. The more time you spent building them, the less time you ever devoted to getting to know the one person you forced to live inside them. You have become so good at protecting without knowing neither why, nor who you are protecting.

You know much about so many and very little about your own self. You spent so much energy in learning things in great detail about so many others that you never found the time to learn something more about yourself. So you became the mercenary of your ambiguity, a soldier who doesn't care who she is fighting for, as long as she is fighting and getting paid, as long as she is able to transform her thirst for blood into money on a daily basis, letting her hopes turn into blood before they turn into currency. Your payment is the distortion of the image awarded to you by the mirror's intelligence during the last time you stare at it near the end of the day, before you turn off the light, revoking its right to judge you. You like feeling like a winner even though you don't know who you defeated.

You like feeling like a winner even though that gives birth to a certain sadness inside you which, because you don't want to recognize it as yours, and even worse, you can't identify it if you see it before you, you end up giving it a strong push so it won't appear in the mirror when the next time comes for you to glance into it before you go to sleep. You really feel the need to push it even more into the deepest parts of your abyss, where all those emotions you don't intend to ever visit live, unless your next melancholy ordered you to. You like to feel as if you are more blindingly bright than real, since you no longer mind feeling phony, as long as you can convince the next darkness you meet to take a step forward and shine the way you taught it, and your previous truth to take a step backward and thus not be able to force you to express yourself the way she taught you.

NADIA: Speaking of shining, would you mind if I left with you the piece of the sun that belongs to me to look after for a few hours? *(Visibly disturbed, she opens the door and walks to her room)*

PARIS: When a soul's various suits of armor end up fighting against the magic tricks used by the ambiguity of her owner, a person realizes that he is made of a piece of sorrow which doesn't know where it is coming from and a piece of joy which doesn't know where it is going. It seems to me that today the authenticity of our life decided to give away all its weaknesses to the first lie that passes before it that isn't able to look it in the eyes without blushing. The sunbeam is not ready yet to forget that it may have hidden still another smile inside it, possibly the one it once stole from the sky when he wasn't watching, to use it during the one time in its life it really won't know how to be brilliant.

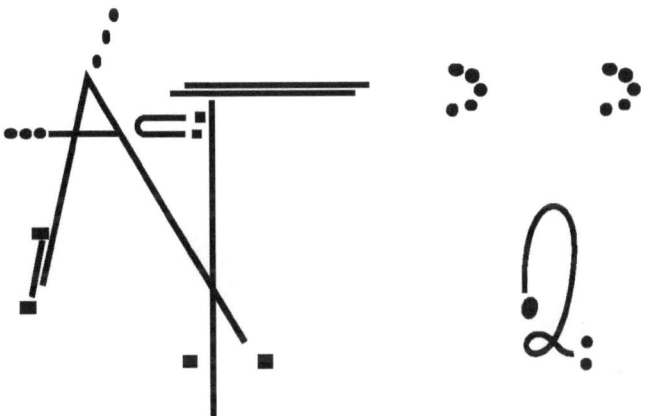

(In the living room, Mother is sitting on the couch talking with Paris and Nadia)

MOTHER: How wonderful it would be if there were sorrows that wanted to die only once! How wonderful it would be if there were emotions that did not insist everytime to make a mistake! How I fear those days when I cannot figure out what my emotions are trying not to tell me, doing their best to avoid looking me in the eyes, not out of shame but out of disgust. I am really irritated by those mysterious full stops which the tired midnight hours carry on their back, the ones that rush to enfold me in the night's first inelegant question a minute before the biggest insecurity of the day that's just ending finally decides to go to sleep and the smallest self-confidence the day about to begin hopes to have when she wakes up. *(The door opens and the Father comes in from work)* Welcome home. Rough day, was it?

FATHER: Rough for my ego, easy for my scream.

MOTHER: What do you mean? What happened at the office?

FATHER *(Leaves his briefcase on the floor and sinks into the couch)*: Nothing really, just the same old routine. I am quite confused. The people around me seem to get more lax day by day, becoming more adept at hiding their good qualities behind their spectacular shortcomings. They are really inclined to lose the symmetry of their own life, rediscovering their beloved asymmetry which their own cowardice knows how to bestow on their image, thus ending up demanding more from everyone else while they are willing to give back as little as they can to the reality they live in. I can no longer watch people that seem to be sleeping while standing on their feet rolling around their own bodies until they find each day's most comfortable spot to rest from too much resting. I don't know… I often catch myself observing a young person and hating him without knowing why.

MOTHER: Perhaps because he has the only thing that we can no longer acquire, perhaps because he enjoys an easier, more comfortable life that the one we had at his age? Are you sure you don't envy him more than you hate him?

FATHER: I see them all parading daily before their plastic happiness, their nominal happiness, armed with dreams that perch on minds that can still fool their owners, making them believe that they have some future in them that they have not seen yet. Why would someone want to make his dreams smarter than himself?

MOTHER: Could they have done it to protect their self-confidence from the next defeat that is coming from afar dressed as a draw? Why would someone prepay with his merits for the mistakes which his shortcomings will soon make on his behalf?

FATHER: It might be even harder to prepay using his fake dreams, the one's he knows won't ever be realized because he doesn't intend to sweat in order to make them happen. I see young people grab their hopes by the waist and dance deliriously happy, showing off their great strength, their youth, without missing the chance before leaving to pierce the dead center of my age with another of those arrow-like stares that demand to be more like ruthless conquerors than innocent explorers.

I see them exercising their butts and their laziness in the coffee shops, where they go, having first almost convinced themselves and certainly everyone else that, since they haven't yet failed completely, they must have achieved something today, they just don't know what. They christen every defeat a draw and every draw a victory that hasn't learned yet how to realize that it won, and so end up sitting on their dreams all day so they don't have to look at them.

Let's not forget that dreams that seek to remain almost invisible can easily fit into any drop of sweat that no longer wants to sweat, hopes that seek to fill their own bodies with holes so they can sink before they reach the future can easily fit into any life that does not want to find out where the limits of its cowardice end and where the next mistake begins. They say, correctly, that the zero which is born out of a man's laziness, wants no other number before it. *(Pause)* We actually worked when we were young, we worked really hard... Not like them. Look at them, they look as if they were born with both their hands raised!

MOTHER: Every generation has its own white silences to defeat, its own black clouds to learn how to push to another part of the sky, before it pronounces him blue.

FATHER: Don't get started again...

MOTHER: Every generation must prove to the previous one that it can defeat the darknesses it created out of the echo of the dreams it did not dare to dream. Come now, let's be fair. It's not the fault of the children that live on a flat plain which we ourselves, as soon as they were born, rushed to empty of all the sheer drops that used to exist there for ages, so as to provide them a life more comfortable than our own, hoping that this way we could convince ourselves that we achieved something.

FATHER: So where did we put those sheer drops my dear woman?

MOTHER: I am afraid that we dumped them inside us. They are the ones that put the words you just uttered in your mouth today.

FATHER: The only thing that makes me feel that ultimately there is some justice is that laziness has an incredibly insidious way of causing its owner a lot more misery than hard work does.

MOTHER: I agree. A life's empty hours give birth to huge holes inside their owner, holes whose iron bars his own boredom has filed to entertain itself seeing him fall through them.

FATHER: I see so many young people walking in the street with a gaze that is empty of life, empty of dreams, empty of tomorrow. Tell me something; how can a life be full and acquire a meaning if the person living it has killed all the dreams he once had inside him? How?

MOTHER: When one's life isn't filled by the future, his insecurities come from all its undefended sides and fill it instantly with yesterday.

FATHER: I see all around me a new kind of beggar, a kind of upscale beggar, young people who have everything, yet have nothing, youngsters who with every one of their breaths beg for charity from their own future.

MOTHER: Upscale beggars… They probably beg for charity from their ambitions too, so they will help them figure out what their future wants from them.

FATHER: What the hell? Are their minds unable to produce anything else except increasingly well made new shortcomings, increasingly well made theatrical sets that know how to hide their mistakes behind their draws? It seems to me that this generation rushed to fall in love with the draw before they went out into the world to try to experience any other outcome. I often see them getting drunk on the remains of their logic, until they start vomiting truths that can no longer bear to be true, honesties that can no longer bear to be honest, realities that can no longer bear to be part of a tomorrow that is afraid to ask yesterday for the opinion it has of its owner. Dazzling ruins, vain ruins! What kind of tomorrow can they deliver? The only thing they can deliver in the future is a blurred photocopy of what they could have been, a shiny but disintegrating success which they began to repair before they even started manufacturing it. By god, was there ever another generation that was so afraid of touching its sweat as much as this one?

MOTHER *(Moves closer to him on the couch and hugs him)*: You're right. This is the revenge of a drop. In life, if you don't sweat today you will shed many more tears later. But come now, calm down. You are tired. Let the young people dream the dreams that suit their strength and come near me so we can dream those that suit ours.

NADIA: Dad, I would really like to tell you that you're wrong, that you don't know what you're talking about, but I hesitate. It would be so good for my ego if I could, and would even offer it some relief for a while. I could say it but as soon as I did, my self-criticism would call me to the corner to scold me without saying a word, just by looking into my eyes, demanding from me to say the one word which all this time I've been doing my best not to utter. I must admit that I cannot, because I know that above all I am one of those people who refuse to absolve the pages of their lives that are still unwritten.
(Irene comes down from her room. She walks for a minute taking very slow steps, as if she is pondering where she will place each one around the room, mumbling to herself something inaudible) You know, we young people refuse to exonerate those dreams our authenticity continues

to dream without our permission, the ones that still haven't found a way to learn how to be disappointed when they are finally forced to reach their finish line and break ahead of us the tape of the reality in which we live. These are the dreams that don't know how to write without our help our emotions on the walls of those hideouts which our own mind has constructed within it to protect us from its own dreams. It's the ones it dreams whenever it finds the strength to tear away from our mediocrity and stand higher, about a courage higher, at that spot in a person's mind where a thought will choose to place itself at least a hope away from his mouth.
(Turns to Paris) You know, a day before we got married, I married the silence contained in a question I never dared ask myself. In the drawers of a marriage that seeks to be as ear-shattering as ours, we learned how to hide every morning in the dawn's first hesitant steps the exhausted darknesses which for years were etched deep inside us by every newly failed attempt to tolerate touching one another's compassion, while deftly avoiding to awaken each other's logic. Our dam wedding from the very first instant loved the total slavery it could easily rent from the neighboring reality in which we lived whenever it wanted, more than any small fragment of freedom, we knew we had inside us but never did anything to own it.

PARIS: Each time one's meanness defeated the other's kindness, this smallest truth of ours would sit for hours at the edge of our marriage and, mad with joy, would take hold of one of the pieces of wreckage itself had just left behind and start drawing its triumph in detail on the loser's gaze. That's how one's dream fought with the boredom of the other to figure out a way to teach him how to become better at getting bored. It's incredible how fast egos, if properly asked by their owners, can rewrite the less glorious pages of their life before the next reality has time to read them and start correcting them.

(Alexander comes down from his room and sits on one of the two armchairs. As soon as she sees him, Irene turns her gaze on him)

IRENE: And we, somewhere between what we experience and what we think we deserve to experience, are looking to find the details of our marriage which, without asking us, with an amazing consistency manages to give birth to a sunset and a fresh defeat in that beautiful fake box where our life stores the mistakes we made together, a box that, overly excited, bring to us soon after as a gift. Disappointed that once again we weren't able to get to know them before we began to destroy them, we walk downhill towards those recently reconstructed hours of our life about which we eventually succumbed to our boredom's proposal to take them from us and sell them to our greed.

Hope stopped long ago trying to figure out why she is the only one that can bear sitting with us at the breakfast table every morning. Our exhausted companionship is searching to find a novel way to plant another rusty smile in the ground, to be trodden by the next common stride of two people who the only thing they can stand to ask their marriage anymore is to replace reality with a memory which, though half broken, occasionally still spews out moments of a kind of joy that insists on being semi-transparent.

NADIA: For a marriage to survive, not just one but both must stop taking out of the most inhospitable drawers of their hearts pre-worn happinesses and keep on throwing them to the wild beast of their rage to devour and feel satisfied for a while until it gets hungry again.

PARIS: You make me feel as if the most skilled acrobat of my soul is about to be betrayed by his love for the void.

IRENE: Who knows, he might discover that he can't live without that emotion he feels every time he lowers his head and sees the void below him looking love-struck into his eyes.

ALEXANDER: Is there a logic that wants to deliberately make an error while counting?

NADIA: Is there a watch that doesn't want to tell its owner the right time?

ALEXANDER: Sure, the same way there is a precipice that knows how to give birth from inside it to its own railing to protect the people that will love it more than they love their own cowardice.

IRENE: Don't trouble yourself, stop trying so hard, move aside and let your ego come talk to me.

(Father gets up, makes a gesture with his hand as if erasing everything he heard and leaves without saying anything. He goes up to his room to watch TV)

ALEXANDER: I will cover each and every tear I will shed, the tears only you out of all the people in the word will be able to see, with this silver silk that my heart will unfold from within her so I can't see, or even feel, my pain not losing even briefly its courage, not yet disappointed at all. The acrobat we are talking about is ready to perform his closing, most impressive number, using only the one sunbeam my sky has whose light will never be able to figure out what my optimism has been avoiding to show me for so long.

IRENE: I am curious to find out, out of all that you told me, what more than I did the darkness, which a few minutes ago came and sat just behind my greatest insecurity and is eavesdropping on us, understood.

ALEXANDER: Please, don't you dare lay a hand on my fears before I tell you to. I will let my heart get up and go sit in the middle of the room, at an equal distance from both of us. I will let her completely uninfluenced to feel for herself, not for me, free to come and go as many times as she wants in and out of my world, until she has managed to listen to all the different kinds of breath I have, until she been able to touch every last poorly lit corner of my life that hasn't decided how close it will let me get to it. And if my heart decides to kick over the bucket with the gray paint with which I have forced her to paint any minute of my life that has yet to decide what color it wants to be, so much the better. I am ready to risk it all, letting herself decide in the end which part of my life she wants to kick away from me and which part she wants to keep.

IRENE: And if she decides not to return to you?

ALEXANDER: It will be okay!

IRENE *(Impressed)*: Wow, that's some strength you got there!

ALEXANDER: By god, I wish she would grab any color she wants and force my normality to exit the main room of my life banging the door behind her, leaving me even for few moments free to decide how normal I can afford to be.

PARIS *(Interrupting them)*: I am tired of constantly adapting to the dimensions the people around me want me to have, cutting a bit here and adding a bit there, measuring all my character traits in quantities that are pleasing to everyone but me. I am tired of being the one who every morning takes a huge eraser in hand and wipes out who I am, deleting my qualities one after the other, until what is left after a while complies with the specifications of the herd I belong to. I am tired of letting them determine how far I can stray from the ideal quantity of any trait of mine without feeling that I am betraying it.

ALEXANDER: I can't stand letting the people around me send those mercenary arguments of their sorrow into me to invade my mind unopposed and nail on its surface the prescribed limits within which my thoughts must move from now on. Why do I let them build a prison in my head whose iron bars are my very own thoughts that didn't dare be born more courageous, the ones that never learned how to get up from the incredibly comfortable couch of "maybe" where they permanently live, the ones that can no longer think for themselves, let alone for me? How did they manage to convince me that, to live happily I must first build a prison in my mind to hold those thoughts of mine that dare to differ from theirs, the ones they consider dangerous, not because they might harm me but because they might harm the person they want me to be?

IRENE: I hear you and I feel that ten fears cannot fit in the first word I so need to tell you, nor in the first thought I want to think, not even in the version of my mind I wanted to wear this morning.

PARIS(*Gushing*): I wish I could guess what my fears are trying to hide from me, which part of myself, which part of my future they want to put in my next sadness before I even get to introduce myself to it and thus gain the right to love or reject it.

ALEXANDER: I wish I could guess what midnight wants from me when it comes dressed as a beggar and stands outside the entrance of my logic waiting for me to go out and offer as charity the part of myself I need most.

NADIA: Paris, hearing your heart overtaking me and already communicating with my own without me being able to intervene, I feel as if my life is flooded with a strange kind of light, a light that just decided that it loves darkness more than its own rays. I like this feeling that only this light can produce inside me so much that, to be honest, I am starting to get a bit scared.

IRENE: I always illuminated the world around me with this enormous floodlight my ego had given me as a gift when I was twenty. Wherever I pointed it, whatever I saw, somehow those desires of that teenage happiness of mine I left unfulfilled were always rushing to get in the middle of the picture.

ALEXANDER: Is this perhaps how you enveloped your every joy, and possibly your every day, with the appropriate pretexts you found resting on the edge of your lips, waiting for you to save them from your reality?

IRENE: Possibly.

PARIS *(Ignoring what the others are talking about)*: How can I satisfy my ego's demands when it refuses to tell me what they are?

IRENE: What are you telling us? That I must start apologizing to my soul for all those questions I hesitate, or rather I am scared, to ask her?

PARIS: I think she is trying to tell you that she wants you to apologize for all those inarticulate cries you have been feeding her for breakfast every day, the ones you hope she will try, with no help at all from you, to transform into words that the people you love can understand, without ever being able to realize which part of your soul these screams were before they were born.

NADIA: Knowing you, I would say that you mean which part of your soul you neglected to insert into what you just said.

IRENE: I don't know, but, if you don't have anything else to do, open a silence and throw yourself in it. You are like the smallest cloud in the sky that hasn't learned yet how to properly hide behind the bigger ones, so that the wind won't separate it and send it into exile, far away from its friends.

PARIS: Come on now...

NADIA: It seems to me that I might just have bought the sky's only two remaining holes, hoping I might hide my shyest virtue in the first, so that I won't feel it anymore, and in the other my loudest scream, so I won't hear it no matter how loud it screams.

ALEXANDER: Why do you want to hide one of your virtues away from you anyway?

NADIA: Because by always keeping in the back of my mind that whatever I do in my life must be consistent with my past I have destroyed entire pieces of my future.

PARIS *(With a questioning look in his eyes)*: Why do you want to do good to your past by hurting yourself? I don't get it.

NADIA: You don't get it? What don't you understand? That once in a while the most powerful weapon I have in my arsenal decides to turn its very bullets against me? Don't you realize that the strongest floodlight a person has at his disposal can sometimes, without any warning, turn and with one glance, just a quick glance, blind him forever?

PARIS: Because you are not handling it yourself?

(While watching TV the Father's face reflects the phrases spoken by the actors in it)

ALEXANDER: Don't you understand that a person's virtues, precisely because they are his strengths, are able to abolish for a while some of his shortcomings from the space where he lives, like the big cities that banish the stray dogs and the homeless before their extravagant, glittery celebrations, installing them somewhere else, usually some point way back in their past which their facade finds no reason to visit.

Thus we temporarily manage to impress ourselves by the total absence of our shortcomings, without realizing that no mind has at its disposal good enough magic tricks to consistently remove its own weaknesses from the visual field of any conversational partner, especially when it is trying to conceal them at a rate that is faster than the birth rate of new ones. The only thing it manages to do is to simply move them to another part of its owner's life, a place where, because it is not so visible, they don't embarrass him as much.

(Shouting) Damn stray dogs of my soul! You are the first thing I see in the morning as I wake up when I have nothing else to see. Damn sorrow! You are the first thing I feel in my life when I have nothing else to feel! You are the first to rush over to hug me, when you see me lying on the floor of reality, hit straight in the face by one of your favorite punches, while you're enjoying seeing all my other emotions standing frozen around me, each one trying to hug the part of me it fears less, having no idea what to do to help me.

PARIS: That's right. No matter how hard I look around me, most times I cannot see my sorrow, which is lurking just a few emotionally hollow moments away! There is probably no other emotion as multi-talented or capable as her within us!

ALEXANDER: There is. The sorrow of the person next to you. *(Long pause)*

PARIS: I didn't want to hear this…

NADIA *(Looking at Paris)*: I am ready to entrust my sorrow to the freshness of your truth because I can no longer stand touching the nakedness of my own all alone. I need a soul's generous kindness by my side, to help me navigate those sections of my meanness' advice that have a gold cover. It is these the words of advice that midnight often ends up leaving outside my door wrapped in its most vulnerable darknesses, before it finally allows me to enter the coming day for the third time today.

ALEXANDER: I've felt that too. I really have…

NADIA: When my other character traits have abandoned me and only my malice can bear to stand by me, I start walking without a specific destination in mind on the road my loneliness has carefully paved with thorns made from a kind of velvet that demands to be more offensive than smooth. Without anyone's help, a few hours later, having first picked them up one by one from its surface and carefully wrapped them around my body, I will end up dancing closely with the one question the dawn pulled out of itself a few hours ago and gave me as a gift. So I will try to run as fast as I can to avoid being grabbed by the rampaging questions posed to me by those parts of the previous day to which I promised that I will do my best not to remember that I ever lived in them.

PARIS: It seems to me that the version of yourself you used yesterday just asked you to give it back the shield it gave you as protection against the gifts that tomorrow's version of yours might bring. *(Pause)*

MOTHER *(To Alexander)*: My son, does your unhappiness have a homeland?

ALEXANDER: What do you mean?

MOTHER: Did you ever try to understand the rules of that game you used to play with your unhappiness, the game in which you have to compete against her without knowing exactly what you have to do to win?

ALEXANDER: I hope you're not talking about that game…

MOTHER: Yes, I am.

PARIS: What game is that, tell me about it, I don't seem to know it.

ALEXANDER: It's the game in which, every time I play, the referee is the latest insecurity that has invaded my mind demanding to let it sit in its center so it can determine thereafter which thought of mine is legal and which isn't, which one can proceed to my mouth and which will have to go with its head lowered to the backside of my mind and throw itself into the trash.

PARIS: I don't think I would like to…

MOTHER: Do you realize that all I have learned about myself I have learned from the fights between the only sunbeam in my life that still believes in me and the one darkness that believes in me even more?

ALEXANDER: Do you know that no matter where I find myself around the world, my melancholy can find me in a matter of seconds if she so chooses, making me instantly feel as if I am not where I think I am, that the moment I am experiencing does not belong to me, thus denying me the right to simply enjoy it?

NADIA: In my life I always got as far as where my biggest, most repulsive shortcoming took me, this cunning mirror of my life that is often more intelligent than me, the mirror my rage likes to stare at moments before she comes out of my body and, enchanting its victims for a few seconds with her otherworldly aura, starts destroying them one by one. Have you ever felt, as if you are the only slave that your own freedom wants to own?

IRENE: Yes, yes I have.

PARIS: Me too, me too... I have felt my dam rage not only want to defeat the very happiness of the person she just defeated, but demand to rip it out from inside him, raise it as high as she can and, holding it in her hand for a while, force me to feel how repulsive her strength is.

MOTHER: I have never met a rage in my life that is satisfied only with trying to destroy the people around her, without feeling the need, once she had done that, to turn against her own owner and make him suffer too.

IRENE: That's why in my life I never took a step beyond the point where my logic felt comfortable letting me see her completely naked, not wearing any of the usual clothes I have chosen for her to put on. You see, I always wanted to avoid upsetting that part of my logic that made me feel that I become more ambiguous seconds before I start being cowardly.

ALEXANDER: You mean the part of our logic that makes us feel more stainless steel than rusted?

IRENE: No, I mean the part that makes us feel more stainless steel and sad than rusted and cheerful.

PARIS: So you shouldn't wonder why I became the shining gladiator of my rage, the person who will defend her to the death each time someone dares to insult her honor.

MOTHER *(To Alexander)*: You know, with your father we both lived an entire life immersed in the questions of a marriage that never cared to learn in what order to write its pages. We lived for years sitting next to each other, each embracing the part of the others' logic he understood best and the part of his own silence he understood least.

ALEXANDER: I would say that, if it weren't for your own tremendous patience, you both would have often been under the impression that you were siting opposite each other, even when you were sitting side by side.

MOTHER: Perhaps, perhaps… Anyway, we always tried, in the heart of the first day of winter that was hidden in the last part of each day that ended without having understood why it began, to let the overwhelming emotional ambiguity each of us felt explain to us what our roles would be in the play our life would stage the next day.

PARIS: Why do I get goose bumps, I wonder, every time I touch my ambiguity, especially when I see it so afraid to come near me and talk to me?

MOTHER: You mean, the nakedness of what you are or of what you feel?

PARIS: The second one. You know, I stopped long ago feeling ashamed for all those emotions I no longer know how to feel. I let them all free to go where they want, being utterly unable to do anything to convince them to stop exploring the spots inside me that want to hurt without having previously asked my permission and, most importantly, without having explained to me why they want to make me feel miserable. I let them free, without interfering, to confess to my fist everything they don't want to tell me.

NADIA: I think that is the way a person learns how to ignore the icebergs he creates himself.

MOTHER: Perhaps, when he stops painting them white.

NADIA: So he can see them better?

ALEXANDER: Probably to convince himself that they are something else, something much less dangerous.

IRENE: I have the impression that we often end up tossing, as deep as we can, at the end of each of our sorrows a gold coin into our soul, so we can't see it, so it won't remind us how radiant we can be. Same with me. This gold coin is trying for the umpteenth time today to teach me how to not feel ashamed about my own radiance, snatching from the sun's hands the first available sunbeam and starting to spread it over my body, to show it how to feel again the brightness, the value it once had. The air between us is ready to take into its arms those endless hours of our life we covered in silence all that we never found the courage to cover in words. It really wants to turn it into the song of two hearts that hand-in-hand will lay siege to the part of their truth that lives in the charity they seek from their common future.

MOTHER *(Turning towards Irene)*: I hope you noticed that tonight the moonlight did not want to give up, insisting so much on walking until it reached the last question of the day, where those realities in your life which darkness could never make you understand, will soon awaken. It is looking to find the one move you don't realize you hide inside you, which will help you slip through your shoulders and get out of who you are, so you can become both the silence of your cowardice and the echo of your courage. The poor thing wants to help you avoid becoming a person who will hear them both following you all day a few feet behind you, trying to pick up any piece of yourself you consider to be at the same time extremely worthless and extremely valuable. It is those pieces of yourself that you discarded on your way, executing to the letter the commands of your mind, which never stopped arguing with your soul about the value it wants to assign to you.

ALEXANDER: You are right. The moments in my life when I felt more confused and unhappy were those during which my mind decided to throw into the trash whatever my soul considered her most valuable possession.

PARIS: My past really irritates me every time it comes into my life uninvited, just to make sure that I still remember how to make my next serenity hate me anytime I feel like it!

ALEXANDER: Especially before you extend your hand to introduce yourself to your next storm.

IRENE: Because the dam past knows that behind the back of every "maybe" that comes out of your mouth you have hidden a small piece of your last mistake's eternity, a simple proof that each time you assume that you are better than the smartest zero you have in you, you end up transforming yourself into the one question posed by the distance between the most fantastic dream your scream is already dreaming and the most realistic nightmare your most cheerful insecurity insists on having.

ALEXANDER: Do you perhaps end up this way becoming the only smile of yours that will never be interested to learn how to smile whenever you want it to?

MOTHER: It is a rough day when a person decides to start wrestling with his silence.

IRENE: It is even rougher if he decides to teach her how to express itself.

NADIA *(Looking tenderly at Paris)*: Hearing you talk, I am trying to visit for the second time a thought borne of your words in the middle of my mind during an argument we had long ago. But no matter how hard I try, I am unable to do it. The main long downhill in my mind sees all the uphills next to it gasping for air trying to understand why life is harder for them and bursts out laughing. For some reason that I don't know, I was always ready to compromise with all that I forced myself throughout the years to fear before I tried to help myself understand it. I don't know… How much courage, I wonder, does a road have which, believing that it should not go on, should never reach where it was told it must end, takes the biggest knife it can find and cuts its own body in two so it won't ever reach its final destination?

ALEXANDER: More courage than a parcel of land that decided to never become a road.

IRENE *(Sits in the other armchair)*: Maybe. I don't know… I only know that I really need to go sit next to this road, embrace it and ask it to give me a piece of the courage its optimism has, a piece of the faith its dignity has.

MOTHER: Please, let me grab the weight of my conscience by the arm and go sit right next to the one emotional currency my past has been using to buy me off from all the fears I have about anything that might happen to me in the future. I hope that today I will finally manage to let the magnificence of my vagueness negotiate with it about how much happiness it will allow the next hour of my life to have. *(She spins around as if wanting to see what she is thinking of saying from a different perspective)* Why do we constantly have to make our joy feel guilty, as if she has done something wrong to displease us?

ALEXANDER *(Interrupting her)*: Because you have forced your happiness to constantly keep company with the only part of your soul that has the ability to give birth to your tears.

NADIA: There are times while I am speaking when only my conversational partner understands what I am saying, while I don't. The more personal the things I mention are, the less I understand what I am trying to say. As the conversation progresses, I feel less and less comfortable with what I am saying, with what the inadequacy I feel is pushing me to say, as if someone else who barely knows me has climbed into the middle of my mouth and is selecting which words will stay inside and which will come out of it. It's so disappointing to hear my own words, as soon as they are done expressing what I have forced them to say, rush to the ear of the person I am talking to and whisper something I cannot hear. *(Pause)* I just hope it's not the truth.

ALEXANDER: It probably is…

IRENE: I have felt that too. Often those words that end up coming out of my mouth know a truth more than me.

ALEXANDER: And those that decide to stay in, one truth less?

EIRINI: Maybe, maybe…

PARIS: I get really frustrated sometimes when I hear my next word breathing hard while rushing down the stairs from my mind to my mouth. Panic stricken, I wait for its meaning at the dock of my mouth to come get me out of the mire I feel and take me to that part of my freedom which has long been asking me to let it live away from me. It's so strange, while you are supposed to feel like the master of yourself, as soon as you start talking, to feel that you are transforming into your inadequacy's slave, an emperor slave who has sold all his life's freedom to his next sorrow.

ALEXANDER: Sometimes I wonder if a person who is the slave of his own soul has more freedom than a person who believes that he is the emperor of his logic.

IRENE: You mean an emperor who ends up being the slave of others?

NADIA: I guess you mean someone who is a slave of his own self.

ALEXANDER: No, I mean someone who doesn't know how to free himself from his own success.

PARIS: Do you have someone in mind?

ALEXANDER: Yes, I do, and I think you know who…

NADIA: May I ask you something? When do you think that our souls will discover the freedom concealed in those emotions which our logic hasn't let us feel all these years, hiding them each time they happen to look elsewhere?

MOTHER: Your kindness does her best to not concede that even at the farthest point inside it for years now she has been hiding a quantity of meanness she is very proud of without knowing why.

NADIA: Who knows, we might have dumped so many darknesses inside us that, when they get together and start talking to each other, they might be able to inadvertently give birth to a sunshine that is more blinding than real.

ALEXANDER: Are you trying to say that a silence is able to make its own words which have a different sound, a different meaning than our own?

IRENE: Silence probably knows how to generate screams that are much louder than any ones we can produce on our own.

MOTHER: You should know, my children, that silences are more cunning than the craftiest word in our vocabulary. They know how to make from scratch whole hours full of these incredibly insidious sounds which they always have at their disposal, sounds that refuse to carry the meaning we want to give them, allowing themselves to insert in them any meaning they want. So, having managed to fool us into believing that these hours are completely our own, they hand them over for us to store in the roomiest warehouses of our mind until the next time we might need them.

ALEXANDER: You mean the next time we fight.

MOTHER: Take it any way you want.

NADIA *(Embracing Paris)*: Our sadness tonight will not hurt herself walking barefoot on any stars that decide to cover the sky with those questions of ours which our egos intentionally left unanswered before we fell asleep so that our minds won't have the time to answer them.

ALEXANDER: You mean before…

MOTHER: Come now, stop that…I have watched you both for days circling around the untold melancholy you have been constructing together for some time now, putting one meanness on top of another, doing your best to not understand what your next happiness is shouting from your life's opposite sidewalk. Have you realized that most of the minutes of your life during which you found yourselves next to each other not knowing what to do to enjoy them, decided after a long while to revisit you? They won't so much to try to traverse the new reality you are offering them, the one which, tired by the superhuman effort to please you, has sat down between you, out of breath and almost unconscious.

I want so much to just make you talk, to each other to make each one of you grab by the hand the most toxic, the most treacherous word with which you could beat each other, and drag it to the entrance of your soul so she can touch it and feel the pain that it has inside it. Forgetting that a body does not belong exclusively to its own expectations, your bed, defeated once again by your awkwardness, will start measuring at midnight the extent of the dreams your bodies are dreaming during those nights when they manage to sneak out and move even just a few inches away from their owners, to give themselves a chance to dream whatever they want.

(Alexander and Irene become extremely nervous, stand up and start pacing back and forth in the living room) Can't you see that, as time goes by, these dreams choose to become smaller, retreating from the well-dressed insecurity of a love which has gotten out of bed, moved two worries away and stands before the only window in the house through which, if you open it in the middle of the night, you can see your past take out of its pockets one by one its favorite highlights of your life? It will carefully prepare them so it has time, before morning, to project them on the movie screen which some of your favorite stars have for some time now crowded together, one against the other, to set up in the middle of the sky just for tonight.

NADIA *(To Paris)*: I wonder, out of all the different kinds of loneliness I feel, how many will ask tonight to sit next to your own to overhear what we say and, as soon as our discussion ends, will try to convince you to enter this narrow corridor in your mind where only a positive thought and a very steep uphill fit to pass through at the same time? Those nasty solitudes are just waiting for a chance to be alone with you to badmouth me to no end!

MOTHER: How many winters will ask to sit next to the promises you made them that you will never find out why every year since you were twenty-two, on the last day of winter you feel a strange urge, maybe even a need, to betray the first day of spring that is coming?

NADIA *(Her head lowered)*: I feel as if I am seeing the first day of summer, ten minutes after it got started, walking towards me pushing aside any person, any wonderful experience it sees before it. After staring at me for a while from tip to toe, with a look that is critical but also strangely compassionate, it grabs me by the collar and drags me, with my feet scraping the ground, all the way to the first day of autumn.

I feel as if the world around me has filled, exclusively for me, with pierced summers, summers that together decided to drill holes in their own bodies so that they won't be able to retain a single day inside them. They let me stare at them for as long as I wish, till I am able to recognize in them the first day of autumn. How the hell have I managed to believe that I am the only person in the world who throws herself into the hole these summers have dug for me until I come out the other side right at the first moment in my life that will refuse to be cheerful?

PARIS: The portable night you never stop carrying with you will not fit into our room today. So gather up the remains of your vulnerability and come along to create with me this summer you so lament.

MOTHER: Can a common future pay all the checks your rage has issued to your past? Have you ever thought why you should be forced to cohabit the same mind with everything your ego fell in love with without your permission?

PARIS: And everything our kindness ended up hating.

MOTHER: Come, sit next to each other, grab the pencil your vanity gave you as a gift and try to draw a pride around the emotional outline your two hearts have already painted on your life's daily routine. Draw a pride that wants to snatch the banner of your relationship from your hands and run to the first square inch of the desert that you yourselves created, which will find the courage to betray all that it was taught and dare bring to life a wildflower from within it.
    Let the pencil free to touch your souls, until it manages to totally absorb all the loneliness they feel, and start painting on the surface of the new day what you would like to dream if you weren't forced to see the dreams your past has ordered on your behalf. I am sure you would really like to be able to feel for the first time in your life how much love you have hidden inside you in places where you no longer know how to search. Face it. Your future does not dream your dreams on your behalf, your past does. Your past is the one that lends you all the materials, or rather all those pieces of yourself, out of which you will be able to build a dream, and then possibly a future.

IRENE *(Sits on the couch)*: Sometimes, when watching a storm approaching from afar while the sky right above me is dressed in the most cheerful and carefree blue it has in its possession, I feel like running out to warn it, to shout to it to try grab as many sunbeams as it can carry in its arms and start running to get away from the evil that's approaching. I feel the agony it will soon suffer, I feel the stress it will experience in the next few minutes, having to quickly find a way to defend itself, to survive.

NADIA: Is the sky's lightning its defense or its attack?

MOTHER: I don't know, but by God I think I see some of its own thunderbolts shed tears realizing what a destructive power they acquire with every minute that goes by.

ALEXANDER *(Sits on the couch too)*: Why do I think that you are talking about the thunderbolts you give birth to inside you and not about the ones that the sky begets?

IRENE: I always thought that people's meanness spawned its eggs in a corner of the sky where the lighting would be born shortly after. Nature cannot contain so much wickedness in it.

ALEXANDER: Do you feel the lightning being born inside you and rising to the sky before it decides to strike the people on the earth?

NADIA *(Tearful)*: I feel that my thoughts are the lighting born in the part of the sky I personally allowed to live in my mind. I can no longer stand to injure the people around me without even touching them. How can a person destroy while believing he is building something?

PARIS *(Moved, he stretches out his hand towards her)*: I don't care if the questions my logic wants to ask our reality see me, I don't even care if my ego sees me refuse to pose them to you. The only thing I want to do right now is to touch your face with my hand, hoping to attract back to my heart those emotions of yours that I don't have enough compassion in me to be able to feel. I want to let them flow through my fingers, hoping they might manage to reach my heart and rouse her, forcing her to make me embrace them.

NADIA *(Raises her head looking at him)*: Will you be able to touch those emotions of mine which my ego knows so well how to hide just before they reach my eyes? Will you manage to recognize them and tell me which ones they are? I want so much to hear from your mouth what those emotions of mine that I don't let my soul feel finally want to tell me, lest I betray some part of myself which my logic has forced me to admire, while at the same time I am really so ashamed of it.

IRENE: I am impressed by how good both of you have become at begging for some chaos from each other's souls to see if it is compatible with your own.

ALEXANDER: You know, maybe when you see in the eyes of the person you love how hard he is trying not to lose each time his ambiguity forces him to wrestle with it...

NADIA *(Interrupting him)*: You see your own chaos becoming more understandable, less chaotic.

PARIS: Perhaps you are right. But please stop taking advantage of the love I have for your melancholy. Stop trying to make her convince me to forgive you.

NADIA: Suddenly my thoughts took a leap and flung themselves in front of the different words that rush around the corridors of my mind at breakneck speed, waiting for me to call them. They are not the words I usually use, but the ones that refuse to pick up any thoughts of mine lying idly on my mind's floor and carry them out into the world, so that they are not forced by expressing them to betray that part of myself I could never figure out what it believes in.

PARIS: The one that always liked to hurt the people you love?

NADIA: Exactly.

MOTHER *(Father enters the living room shaking his head disapprovingly. Mother slowly goes and stands between them so that Alexander cannot see him)*: So tell us, son, tell us!

ALEXANDER: I feel as if this incredible dance move my cowardice uses to avoid encountering the gift my future is preparing to give me is starting to become my rage's favorite method of not letting me realize how angry it is. The great secret never to be confessed to me by the one teardrop I have in me, which always demanded more truth from me than I was actually willing to offer it, wants to become the road that could lead me to happiness. My truth, to avoid betraying those traits of mine I have told her to fear, decided to uproot from the ground the "stop" sign just in front of my life's biggest impasse, hide behind it and wait for me to go through it first.

NADIA: I always thought that "stop" signs were quite humorous.

ALEXANDER: I don't get it.

NADIA: I always considered the way "stop" signs use our fears to show us who we are very amusing.

IRENE: I have to admit that I like the way they instantly produce new insecurities in our heads.

MOTHER *(Turning towards Nadia)*: Come on, turn your fists towards the sky and, after telling it what you have to confide to it, bend down and drop them at its feet so it can pick them up and start beating you with them.

IRENE: I think we have become a couple that can no longer stand fighting against the waves we ourselves create. Let's face it. We have become the most frightened part of each other's truth. As I see us talking, each one facing the other's emotional ambition, I feel that if we add our two hearts together we will get something less than a hope and something more than a sorrow. Adding up our fears we will get something less than an illusion and something more than an inadequacy.

NADIA: What are you trying to say?

ALEXANDER *(To Irene)*: It's time my mind took a step aside and let my happiness answer the questions you want to ask me.

IRENE *(Interrupting him)*: Is our relationship anything more than a moving velvet cage which from the day it was born wanted to have two steering wheels? And what are we but two rookie drivers who both insist on driving it at the same time? It's so incredible to see two people running like maniacs to get into the cage their common sorrow built exclusively for them, as if they won't find a seat if they are late! Why must a marriage's happiness have so many entrances and only one emergency exit?

ALEXANDER: Help me out here…I remember us running to get inside it because we couldn't stand getting rained on by the steel drops of rage which were showered down upon us from those skies that live amidst our two solitudes each time they themselves made love without us being there. We got into our cage because we couldn't bear living outside of it. We got in it because our marriage taught us early on to not let our egos alone for too long, giving them the opportunity to try and devise a strategy on how to conquer our next happiness.

IRENE *(Continues lost in her thoughts)*: Our poor cage is bleeding from the furious blows of our stupidity, because the stupidity that believes in her owner more that in herself is invisible. It's this stupidity that has a way of grabbing our secrets one by one from that part of our mind that wants only to reveal and can no longer stand to hide, cramming them in those memories of ours we no longer know how to remember without using the tools our optimism is not sure whether it is good for us to use. I really hate touching that cursed velvet fence which, just before we start arguing, we both anxiously run to erect to get inside it and protect ourselves from the persons we usually transform into as soon as we start fighting. I think our next fight just came to ask our permission to never return to work again.

ALEXANDER: You think that the uncertainty about our future does not want to end because it hasn't had time to cover up, to hide under its magic cape those emotions we assigned it to take away from us so we can't feel them any longer, or because it's time it confessed behind our back to the first sunbeams of the day where it hid them?

IRENE: I wish I knew!

ALEXANDER: Oh day of mine, forgive me please for what I am ready to do to you.

IRENE: Oh day of mine, forgive me for all that I have already done to you and don't know how to confide to you.

ALEXANDER: Our relationship can fit one lie less than those we want to put into it.

IRENE: I think our bed has learned over time to fit one lie more than those we could stand telling.

ALEXANDER: Maybe even more lies than those we can come up with.

IRENE: Maybe...

ALEXANDER: And certainly more lies than those that could fit in any dream each of our bodies dreamt.

IRENE: All these years I allowed your words to touch the parts of my body you could not. Now I finally realize that a bed that can no longer fit two egos can only fit two sorrows and a separation.

ALEXANDER: Two former truths today become sorrows.

IRENE: Maybe even wings…

ALEXANDER *(Gets up and starts pacing back and forth)*: Is there, I wonder, a moment in a couple's life when each one's inadequacies, refusing to fight among them once again, get up and go away, leaving the couple behind speechless?

IRENE: I am sure there is. Perhaps that day is today. Perhaps our life's mirror will wake up an hour before us today to have time to prepare for what it wants to show us.

MOTHER: Come now children…

IRENE: Maybe today is the day we finally find the key that lives in the middle of every mirror that doesn't know how to tell its owners what it has long been feeling each time it sees them both standing in front of it, waiting to receive those answers from it that, swiftly overtaking reality, know how to soothe first their own arrogance and then their stupidity. I think I see my life already starting to write on my next decision the adventures of a loneliness which for the first time in years can stand being alone again.

ALEXANDER: I think I feel the claws of this loneliness of yours still digging into the softest part of the insecurity I have about the future. *(Pause)* How do you approach again a loneliness you once felt, one you had abandoned for years amid the part of your life you always filled with hundreds of people so you wouldn't feel alone?

IRENE: The same way you approach a word of yours that hasn't spoken to you in years.

ALEXANDER: How?

IRENE: Embracing a thought of yours that up until recently didn't know how to ask your permission to let it be born.

ALEXANDER: Perhaps…perhaps! How though… where will I find the courage to speak to the part of myself I have never spoken to?

IRENE: I am not sure. *(Pause)* Maybe by pushing aside the emotional comfort which for years had become the drug our routine used every morning. This comfort, this cursed comfort that drew so much strength from our persistent reluctance to shed a single drop of sweat in order to discover not who we are when we function as a couple, but who we can become if both of us step aside and start living separately from each other.

ALEXANDER: I feel as if all my screams today want to suddenly throw away the shields and spears I forced them to constantly hold in their hands. The poor things had shouldered all these years the burden of not only defending me whenever my insecurity needed them but also of attacking each time my arrogance asked for their help. Today is the first time they are ready, after first spitting me in the face, to rush at each other and start embracing.

IRENE: Yes, the pockets in which the night kept its best built darknesses all these years suddenly decided to open holes in themselves and let them free to leave, to be liberated and to liberate.

ALEXANDER: Are you frightened by the blank page which tomorrow will bring tonight at midnight and hold for hours eight inches away from your face?

IRENE: I am very frightened by it, but I am more frightened by the page full of scribbles it forced me to look at every morning it woke me up until now. I don't know, but I have the impression that, when a person is no longer able to love the truth today offers him, he convinces himself that it's time to fall in love with the myth tomorrow will eagerly supply him with. I don't know if this is so, but I really want to try to find out.

ALEXANDER: Does he perhaps fall in love with tomorrow's myth because he realizes that his life's truth refuses to love him anymore?

IRENE: Perhaps.

ALEXANDER: No matter how hard we try to glue together those pieces of our dreams which they themselves return to us unused every morning, we will never be able to build a tomorrow in which we will be able to fit along with them. The false witnesses of my sorrow that lived inside my smile for the last few months, are ready to grab those life-jackets I always leave hanging from the edge of my lips and leap into the void that my next happiness leaves behind when she decides how far away she wants to stay from me.

IRENE: Some hearts drown in their own blood.

ALEXANDER: Some minds drown in their own light.

IRENE: And us along with them.

ALEXANDER: Yes, us along with them… Goodbye "maybe", hello "no more".

IRENE: Goodbye finish line…

ALEXANDER: Hello starting line. *(He suddenly makes a sharp half turn around himself)* When I say goodbye to you I will use the kind of handshake that only knows how to push away the person it greets, not how to bring her close. I won't be saying goodbye just to you, but to a part of me as well. I won't be saying goodbye to a part of my life, but to a part of me that just announced to the whole world that it doesn't want to belong to me anymore. It's the part that, since the day I met you lived within me in a place my soul's hands were never able to reach. I am sorry you're leaving, but I am glad you are not coming.

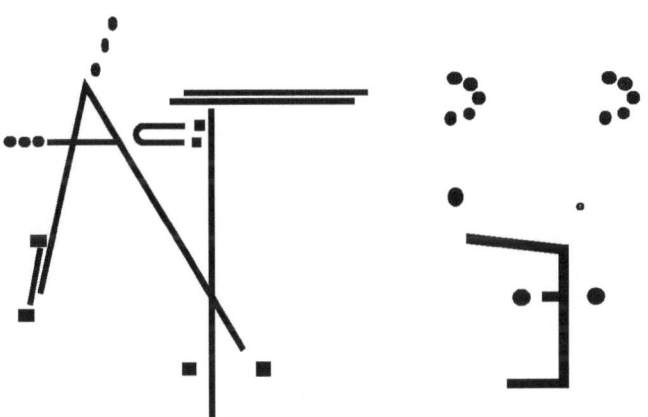

(Sunday noon. In the dining room everybody is sitting at the table)

FATHER *(To Alexander)*: Why should I care if you hold the door for your politeness to go in ahead of you every time you enter a room? What difference does it make to me when you have ended up becoming a black and white photocopy of your courage, the loose change a person gets after paying the bill his real value presented him with, the tip your cowardice gives daily to your hope so she will continue to serve her what you never ordered? If I can't stand something, it's the people that will never find the courage to fight that battle in their life which at its end insists on taking a step forward and start showing them who they really are. Poor unfortunate man, figure out what your value is! Grab your inadequacy by the throat and ask her to tell you your value! You don't deserve your victories, not a single one of them! You don't even deserve the victories I bought for you. *(Lowers his head)* How can you come up daily with a new way to disappoint me?

ALEXANDER *(Calmly, not wanting to antagonize him)*: It would be great if we could lead two parallel lives, a second one to put all our mistakes in, and a first one for all that we do right!

FATHER: How convenient it would be if you young people could break away, escape from what you wanted to become! You would like that, wouldn't you?

ALEXANDER: Today my steps are ready to devour their guilt and then begin to attack their own innocence. I feel compelled, while holding the last tear the night shed on my behalf, the one she brought me this morning utterly disappointed, to start fighting the first delusion I am ready to give birth to in the next few minutes. Father, please give me a word of advice so I can carry on…

FATHER: A word of…

ALEXANDER *(Interrupting him)*: Not the advice you give me to protect your future from me, to shield your dignity from my mediocrity. I won't stand spending another day as the only official guest of your unhappiness. *(Pause)*While we are talking, I feel as if this table, submitting to the commands of your misery, is becoming longer, creating new seating places which are taken up one by one by the unknown to us reasons we are not happy as a family, perhaps the reasons I am not happy. As time goes by, the table keeps filling up more and more, with everyone laughing at each other's jokes and having a good time, except for us.

Nearby I see our melancholy dressed in a beautiful evening gown wandering around the cold room, avoiding to sit with us until the last guest enters. He is the only one I don't recognize, a slightly aged but still gleaming mirror that listlessly walks over and sits right across from me, taking the only seat you had all intentionally left empty. The damn mirror will force me to talk to myself all evening and hours later will get up, come close and, after silently standing right over me for a few unbearably drawn out moments, will bend down, embrace me and brake into tears.

FATHER: What are you talking about?

ALEXANDER *(Stands up to his father for the first time in years)*: Have you ever wondered how many people you have hurt in your life?

FATHER: You mean how many people I have crushed.

ALEXANDER: No, I mean how many you have hurt.

FATHER: By winning you hurt your opponent. *(Pause)* You would know that if you won more often.

ALEXANDER: Try to feel the pain your pain feels. You will feel better when you stop spending all your time surrounded only by your victories, listening to them tell each other every conceivable detail of your triumphs. Push them aside and move deeper into yourself, where the air is not so clear, where the light dares not go because your ego, in order to protect you from your own truth, doesn't let it reach so deep. It's there you have sent all your defeats to live, as if they were lepers, so that you won't have to realize how much less of a winner from what you want to believe you actually are. Move close and let them talk to you until you see them stop cursing you, lower their fists and become serene again, become compatible with the part of your future that will never ask you what you have hid inside the apology you owe it.

FATHER: Nonsense, nonsense. Who has time for such nonsense, such sensitivities? Life is a fist. Who has time for the cuddling and the foolishness I hear you all talking about? Only people who don't really work and are not fighting everyday have time for this nonsense. At your age I had to really, really work. I didn't have the option of sitting around all day, slowly becoming so soft that I became inoperative, worthless. I had to learn, with each passing day, how to be even tougher, more aggressive, so I could bear the pain of becoming better. Every day I woke up I had to be tougher, not like you, a pile of the most useless stuff a person can find in the world, his own cowardice. You are soft because I gave you the right, the option to be as soft as you want.

Ah... Every couch is a harbor that wants to keep the ships in it forever docked. *(Jumps up and starts pacing nervously around the table)* Face it, it's with my money you buy every minute of your life you choose to spend with your cowardice and not your sweat, every minute you choose the security the couch offers you over the risk the next voyage presents. You stay in the safety of the harbor I made for you and talk about how exciting it would be if you were out in the storm doing battle with the elements. Why don't you go out there and see for yourself how great it is to face the merciless attack of those waves made out of steel which life sends straight at you? Why don't you go out there and see how nice it is, under the stress of not knowing whether you will survive, to feel your head drain itself of its own blood the exact moment you have to make the best decision you can to save yourself while your stomach get's worked on by two storms simultaneously, the one you see before you and the greater storm your insecurity spawns inside you every second that goes by?

Go out, why don't you! *(His voice breaks)* Go out of the harbor and see the crushing defeats that live inside every man-eating wave you see before you staring at you with a look that seeks to drain any last drop of courage left inside you, patiently waiting for the right moment to devour you. Have you ever felt the next minute of your life playing seesaw with you, pushing you up and down as if you weigh no more than a leaf? You talk about pain. What the hell do you know about pain, you who, as soon as you hurt a little, don't try to find a solution on your own but rush off, panic-stricken, to buy it from the pawnshop operated by your favorite insecurities?

I'm talking about that horrible place where your chemical friends work, the ones who are always willing to help you feel better for a few hours by destroying who you are, obliterating the reality you experience while offering you another for a short time, a substitute reality, a reality in which they remake from scratch, showing you how to become a present-absentee, a body from which they have managed to briefly extract a piece of its soul, a human being bereft of truth, empty of substance. How much pain can you endure, you who can't stand being alone, really alone, for even ten minutes? Go out into your life, go out so we can all see what you are really made of, go walk around its outer limits, feel the toxic breeze of the unknown slapping you in the face. I am taking about life's real boundary, not this small circle you have drawn around those few virtues of yours that still keep you company so you won't force your self-indulgence to suffer, realizing how significant your capabilities are.

ALEXANDER *(To his Father)*: Sometimes small, insignificant corks survive great storms better than huge, expensive ships. You are a man condemned to live in your grandeur, condemned to live the failure of your own success. Without you realizing it, your fists have long been cursing you behind your back. So stop glorifying your triumphs and listen to what they have to say to you as soon as you turn off the giant floodlights you have been pointing at them day and night. Get it into your head, you great winner, your triumphs have been taking advantage of you for years, while letting you believe all along that you have been taking advantage of them.

By letting you milk your brightness as much as you can so it will continue to supply you with trophies, your victories don't let you realize that each time you manage to win, they have already managed to drink your own blood, drawing the man out of the triumph, the essence out of the illusion, sucking who you would like to become out of who you are, eventually leaving behind a miserable skeleton, an emotional corpse! You have walked thousands of miles in your life wearing a dream next to your skin to which you never gave a few minutes of your time, so you can both stop running and sit next to each other, offering it an opportunity to share with you its own dreams and possibly its own fears. Poor man, did you ever figure out what was in that youthful dream of yours you always wanted to make happen, the one you started chasing at twenty and after a point, when it realized what you were asking it to be, turned around and started chasing you? *(The Father takes a few steps and sits alone on the couch across the room)*

During your life you occasionally bred various types of deserts within you. They all had something in common: they wouldn't let other people reach the oasis that exists inside you so they could drink some water from your own truth. You personally had placed your oasis in a part of your life which you had identified as the desert's end, but it was never there. These are the kind of deserts with which a person surrounds his logic so that his dreams can't touch her, thus protecting her from the hopes his soul once had for him. *(The Father lowers his head and puts it between his hands)* What have you offered me except for a perpetually sad parade of gifts with which you tried to buy my respect, while each time you offered them to me I felt your ego throwing them ostentatiously in my face? The poor things rushed as fast as they could to simultaneously spawn before my astonished eyes two tears for every smile, two hatreds for every fear, giving me all six to keep as a good luck charm. You make me feel like a whore that doesn't want to admit to herself what line of work she is in, a whore who is paid in material possessions to pretend she loves the great benefactor by, unlike the others, always keeping her mouth shut. With every gift of yours you sought to demonstrate to everyone around me that great whores don't live in whorehouses, great whores are the ones keep on living by getting paid to always keep their mouths shut.

Every time you bought off a piece of my soul, my well-being fell in love with you all over again and my ego found a new reason to hate you even more. *(Weeping)* You cannot lift a person up by knocking him down. You cannot kiss him while spitting at him. Every time you opened the shiny box containing each new gift you brought me, the damn thing would jump out and hand to me a sickly cardboard smile and a huge iron shadow, a shadow I could never stand to sit next to even for a moment, no matter how hard I tried. Soon after, that dreadful shadow, after managing to buy off my conscience from my biggest insecurity, would spread all over my body like a virus and, while making love to me, would immediately begin to devour me.

FATHER: What else could I do but offer you everything?

ALEXANDER: You could offer me the highest peak and the deepest abyss in your heart, and stop offering me what's left of a heart that has already spent all her strength training your great triumphs on how to admire you even more. How I wish you would let her show me, even once in a while, her greatest anguish, her greatest fear, so that I too could feel not what you are, but what you're afraid to become.

MOTHER *(Raising her head skywards)*: Dear god, hide me from my thoughts, hide me from the one word my next thought wants to unleash from inside it! Hide me from the part of my past I have charged with paying the bills of my sorrow.

ALEXANDER: Who will protect you from your life's great achievements? Don't you see that with every day that goes by your achievements manage to amputate another part of your soul, making it smaller than it was the day before? Can't you see that every morning, as soon as she wakes up, your melancholy takes you by the hand and brings you to the part of your life where your courage meets the next midnight you have been long hiding inside you? She wants to convince you to put your right hand in your soul, grab that part of hers and, raising it as high as you can, enjoy watching it up in the air, cut off from the rest, cold, deadened, making you feel hundreds of emotional miles removed from life itself, from the compassion, the joy, the passion you feel all around you except for inside you. Don't you see? Your success achieved what she wanted. Have you?

Face it. Your success managed to destroy you. You were destroyed by every triumph in your life which, as soon as it stopped applauding you, began to cut a piece off your compassion and threw it to the wild beasts of your vanity to devour. Don't you get it? For years now you have lost the spare parts of your own truth, with which you are called every night at 11:59 to repair, in just a minute, the happiness of your next day, a happiness which your past has already done everything it could to demolish on your behalf.

FATHER: I feel that today the peak of my life was orphaned. Today, every sinister gaze I met in my life came to rape one by one all the apologies I owe to who I am.

ALEXANDER: Father you have toiled so much, you have fought so hard in your life. Trust your wounds again to tell you who you are. I wonder, have you ever asked your success not if she believes in you, but what she thinks of you? Did you ever ask your success if she herself wanted to succeed? You have been sitting for years on the peak of your life which you built by yourself, holding in one hand your biggest character flaws and in the other the memoirs which your own virtues have written about themselves, standing with your right boot on the head of all the apologies you owe to every mistake you have urged your meanness to make on your behalf. Have you ever thought how much more human, how much more happy you would be, have you ever thought how much closer to us, to me, you would be if you weren't so good at being perfect? By being so good at becoming better you became incredibly good at becoming a worse human being. Your meanness became the very gold medal you never pursued but will gladly accept. So take it, take it and hang it around your neck, and then weep, first out of pride for winning it and then out of sadness for what you allowed it to make of you.

FATHER: Don't prostitute the best arguments you can come up with to convince me that you are somewhat less than smart and something more than innocent.

ALEXANDER: Don't let your own size devour you…

FATHER: You speak of peaks. Which peaks and which triumphs? Face it! I bought for you whichever peak you conquered in your life. With my money, my connections, my sweat!

ALEXANDER: What you managed to show me is that the higher I go, the closer I get to the peak, the more it makes me feel, staring at me with that incredibly forbidding look, as if while ostensibly ascending I am actually descending, as if I am slipping down, making it seem, with every new step, more and more like a deep, bottomless abyss. You are indeed the peak of my life, a peak, however, which I must never conquer because I know that the moment I step on it, the damn thing will have already managed to step on me first.

FATHER: Nonsense, nonsense…

ALEXANDER: What more am I than a mere machine struggling to climb the flight of steps it found already built by others, a ladder whose steps you built yourself snatching my virtues one by one from inside my soul and stacking them one over the other? It's the peak where you took me since I was young every time you saw the sun set two hours earlier for you than for the rest of the world. Without ever asking me, you would take my foot and place it on the first step of the ladder to convince me that it was time to start climbing, time to start conquering.

You made me traverse all my character flaws to reach that point in my life where, as I climbed, I could never see the summit for more than a few seconds, though I felt its critical gaze constantly fixed on me. You never noticed, but following almost every ascent, after we had returned to our life's flatland, I would go back to the spot where I started, dragging behind me any part of my soul that wanted to stay with me and, after gathering any leftover courage I had tossed around my life using my mind's dustpan, I would raise my head up high, look the peak in the eyes and shout at it with all my strength: "Damned mountain, at least let me build the stairway myself, let me construct with my bare hands the means I will use to conquer you."

FATHER: I refuse to fight with you but I will gladly fight with your ego, if you manage to first remove all the phony courage it still wants to hold on to.

ALEXANDER: How did you manage again today with a single move to hide a whole winter in the backside of my self-confidence? I want so much to convince her outmost boundaries to give birth to one word which will not take a single step back, no matter how many times you attack it, no matter how treacherously you strike it.

FATHER: What more are you than a man who is smaller than his own dimensions? A person who is wearing a life whose size doesn't fit his potential because he has dressed his mind with a dream that is one size too small? What more are you than a man living in the middle of his life's dirty ashtray, surrounded by the butts of his own ambition, a person who lives right where his self-esteem extinguishes its own questions one by one every morning so it won't have to ask them?

(Alexander does not respond)

FATHER *(Shouting)*: You have nothing else to say! Now you play dumb? Where did your smart words go, where are they hiding?

ALEXANDER: How many mines will you have to lay in the middle of my smile to be finally pleased today?

FATHER: How many have you planted yourself under the road to your success so you will never manage to cross it?

ALEXANDER: And what is all this about success, anyway? Who told you that I want to succeed in anything? What am I, the son of a king who has to succeed so that the totally corroded, wretched monarchy can continue to exist? How can you expect me to reign supreme in your kingdom when I can't even rule the kingdom of one person, myself? How do you expect me to be the peak when I still don't know how to live happily at the base? When will you realize that I don't want to become the extension of any part of your life, let alone what you are asking me to be, the extension of your unhappiest part, your own shadow?

FATHER: Who do you think I did all this for, for whom did I work so hard all these years? *(Turning towards the Mother)* Tell him, tell him how many terribly steep uphills I had to climb, uphills covered in sweat and rust, littered with dreams and shadows, dreams and shadows… Tell him. Tell him!

ALEXANDER: You did it for me, but most of all you did it for yourself. *(Pause)* Your every word was always a judge, your every silence a brand new prison cell which, as soon as I tried to respond to the accusations already leveled at me by your perfection, would open its own door to lock me inside. I can no longer stand to remove words from what I have been holding back from telling you for so long, and I can stand even less removing silences from it. The time has come for the love and pain I feel for you to meet in every word my soul wants to deliver at your feet, to gather all the courage I have in me and try to talk to you without me being present. I won't let my self-preservation rush off to modify what I have to tell you to get me out of the appointment that time arranged long ago with our truth, perhaps my truth as well. This time I won't let the gentle ambiguity of my survival get between me and my next tranquility.

Today our delusions are sorting out the lies they told all these years in order to daily update the encyclopedia of our common defeat and keep it current. Not only my defeat but yours as well. Because in a family, no matter how dysfunctional she is, when one member loses, when one becomes smaller, all lose, all end up becoming smaller. Face it. It's time we realized that in this battle we both lost, because when a person distances himself from any of the two people that created him, he distances himself from his own self. Without realizing it, he commands his hands to tear into his own flesh and, after splitting his self in two, throw the pieces as charity to his various insecurities of his which for years now haven't stopped following him with hands outstretched wherever he went.

MOTHER: Come now, stop that. I can no longer listen to you tearing into your own skin to plant another wound inside you.

ALEXANDER: What I wouldn't give just to be able to jump back to my beginning and curl up in its warmth and comfort, to try to understand why I ended up becoming the person I was hoping I could never become!

MOTHER: You became who you are because you didn't try harder to not become the person you always hated.

(The Father starts reading a newspaper. He raises it up conspicuously, as if trying to hide himself from the others)

ALEXANDER *(Uncaring, continues to talk alone)*: What can my logic gain from me? I can no longer stand rushing at breakneck speed through the corridors of my mind, astride my most ambitious thoughts, letting them destroy whatever they find on their way without being able to do anything to stop them. My family, please come close to me, everyone, please, come near and strip me of my most bloodthirsty thoughts. I can no longer stand smelling the awful stench of the blood of every thought of mine which demanded to be more ambitious than me, dying on the surface of that dream that has been long waiting for me to dream it.

IRENE *(She can't hold back, she really wants to express what she feels, she really wants to let it all out)*: I feel what you are saying. There are many mornings when I start my day by waking up our common wounds one by one, the ones I see sleeping scattered all over our bed. I wake them up so I can hold them in my hands and start wearing them around my body, promising them that I will take them with me wherever I go during the day. Before I even wish anyone good-morning, I feel a civil war being declared inside me between what I want to become and what the steely general of my life, the so hated "must", commands me to be.

MOTHER: I, on the other hand, while looking inside me, sometimes see my own abyss full of sharp peaks that are ready, the moment I manage to scale them, to let me enjoy for a minute and then, smiling at me, to push me off into the void. And you know, this void belongs to them, not to me, and is incredibly painful because the dam thing, once you're inside it, can make you feel like a complete stranger, a stranger inside your own body.

PARIS: When you have successfully managed to hide from your own truth for so long, you begin to feel that the only part of yourself to which you ought to go whenever called upon are your lies. Damn it, I have felt like that too many times in my life, far too many!

FATHER *(To Alexander)*: Why don't you tell us at what point in your life you began to feel certain that you will never become what you once dreamed to be?

NADIA*(Interrupting him)*: If you want to talk about what we fashioned in our teens at the most velvety, distant edges of our dream, the edges that we visited as rarely as possible because we were really afraid we would taint them with our normality, I am leaving. I won't be able to stand talking about something I don't want to remember again the technique I had to devise to forget it.

MOTHER: Come, take a seat, sit down…

ALEXANDER: You are talking about the time when I dreamed because I wanted to, not like now when I dream each time I have nothing better to do, aren't you?

IRENE: Ah, there was a time when we lived so emotionally close to our dreams that many times we didn't know where the dream we were dreaming ended and where the dream that our reality was dreaming began.

ALEXANDER: Yes, right. At the time we had a very harmonious, very symmetrical relationship with our dreams. They needed us as much as we needed them, they used us as much as we used them. With the power of our imagination in them they were able to come up with all the mental fabrications they wanted, letting us free to use all their optimism to make them real. Now we are not inclined to give them back anything, we just want to take, doing our best to draw every last ounce of positive energy from inside them, because we know that our own reserves of it are almost depleted.

FATHER *(To Irene)*: I didn't know that your ambiguity is so short-tempered.

IRENE: I know her well. You should know that if you want to bend down and tell her a secret she is very discreet, she will never tell.

MOTHER: You should both stop being so fascinated by the part of your serenity that is doing its best right now to not let you define it.

IRENE: I will let my misery come meet you before you put your next phrase into words. *(Pause)*

NADIA *(Gets up and goes to the mirror that is hanging on the wall across from her)*: The first time a person realizes that he is unable to meet the demands of his own dreams, he becomes a smuggler of the authenticity he is trying to sell to his own self-confidence to buy her off so that she will let him feel, even for a short while, that the tranquility he is experiencing really belongs to him. Face it, this is who you have become. *(She moves closer, stretches out her left hand towards the surface of the mirror and touches it as if she wants to experience through her fingers what she feels while looking at it)* Dam you, the time has come for you to confess to me everything you have been doing your best for so long not to tell me. It's time you threw at my feet all the glances I gave you in my life, begging you to start lying to me while urging you at the same time to tell me the truth. It's time you told me how the hell I ended up becoming the thief of my own identity, a person that has to look in a mirror so it can tell her how authentic she can stand to be without starting to become so real that she seems phony. My god, how did I end up becoming a person that broke into her own self to steal what can only belong to her, what has no use, no value for anyone else?

MOTHER: Each day offers us a single opportunity to get to know ourselves. Today I think it took pity on us and will not end before it helps us out a bit more.

NADIA: Each day usually gives us only one precipice to fall off from. I think today it gave us another one as a gift.

PARIS: I don't understand why we must live a life during which we traverse each day with the right to endlessly walk between our sorrow's scrawniest optimism and the most heavily-built pessimism of our joy.

FATHER: Have you agreed which of the two of you will pay the bill your stupidity just presented you with?

MOTHER: Don't say that, don't…

FATHER: No one, because you have both become so good at making your mistakes look more like missteps, to the point where to you they seem almost beautiful. How convenient! How wonderfully foolish!

IRENE (*Turning towards Alexander*): Can you please set up for me an appointment with coincidence? I think that I will really need her today. I think that at midday today, a darkness will leave the part of the world where it is still night and will come sit cross-legged before me, begging me to hug it as tight as I can! While all my insecurities applaud and encourage it, just to satisfy any emotion of mine I don't understand though I have already started reluctantly feeling it, this darkness will spawn within me the rest of its body, that section it never dared until now to admit that it was part of itself. With every minute that goes by it will feel stronger and stronger, so much so that it will scare away every last ray of the sun, until it chases them all away from me. The damned thing won't stop growing unless my sorrow orders it to back off.

NADIA: Why do I have the impression that even the most undisciplined thought you have inside you is a darkness that has become a key that no longer knows how to open doors, only how to lock them? I fear that it may gather speed at any time and start destroying the hope we have inside us, not by striking it but by simply unpeeling it before us, forcing us to re-discover the layers of optimism we created it from, till in the end the only thing that's left is the core that gave birth to it, a skinny whisper which, from the moment it's discovered, will start slowly dying before our very eyes.

MOTHER (*Nodding her head as if in agreement*): Indeed. Every hope I have is a whisper begging me to never teach it how to agree with what my cowardice tells it, how to not bow its head each time she interrupts it and decides to speak up on my behalf. How will I do that? I don't know…I see my life's reality looking at it with that severe, disparaging look in her eyes, and I see the hope in it buckle from the pressure it feels. Sometimes I feel that by now the poor hope has transformed into that darkness of mine which knows how to sail towards the truths of my life I purposefully left undefended without me being able to do anything to stop it, and after finding the biggest and most charming one, strike it like a torpedo, smashing it into dozens of small truths that are doomed to never again recognize each other, so they won't ever be able to reunite and become a courage.

ALEXANDER: I am trying, using only phrases that no longer want to belong to the memory my kindness uses to make me look better than I actually am, to construct a silence which demands to be more insulting than any word of mine. I need her because I feel so defenseless, so unarmed each time I stay alone with that cursed mirror across from me, the one that for now hours has been silently watching every move I make. It is waiting for the right moment to grab any virtue of mine it can from within every word I utter and, as soon as I fall asleep, deliver it to my defeatism in order to figure out, using the information hidden on its backside, new ways it can devise to defeat me.

PARIS: A virtue's backside is sometimes more destructive than the biggest character flaw…

IRENE: Now I understand why we sat across from each other all this time, each one armed with the latest model of loneliness which his own future intends to give him as a surprise gift, fighting without fighting, losing without losing. So, the identity of our common happiness, which I intentionally lost once inside the most cunning serenity I ever felt in my life, loses consciousness, unable to figure out where her own limits end and where the limits of the self-confidence I will use tomorrow begin.

ALEXANDER: So, the identity of our common happiness becomes the identity of our common failure.

PARIS: Oh, I wish I could talk to my self-confidence as easily as you talk to yours.

MOTHER *(To Irene and Alexander)*: Tell me, have you ever truly wondered what you owe to your marriage?

IRENE: Perhaps our authenticity.

ALEXANDER: Don't you agree that our marriage keeps finding new ways to forget what it never wanted to know in the first place?

IRENE: What do you mean?

ALEXANDER: Does every relationship between two people need a little gray in it to be able to survive? Does it need it so it can figure out how valuable that time of night is when white and black decide to embrace each other forgetting their differences? Is that the time when self-confidence becomes more afraid of herself than of darkness, the time that urges both of them to hold hands and stand upright, one on the left, the side the man sleeps on, and the other on the right, the side the woman sleeps on, patiently waiting until both of them wake up in the morning so they can start defining all over again, not only what their marriage means today, but also what its value will be to each one separately?

MOTHER: Yes, the white and black of our lives can be so useful! They are the ones that extract from their own bodies the raw material out of which they make the gray in which we end up spending most of the time during our lifetime. It took me so many years to realize this! I wish I could tell you how to trust the thousands of gifts the gray has given you throughout your life until now, but I can't. I wish I could tell you that the pebbles the gray puts in your shoes every morning, so that you won't be able to feel as comfortable as you'd want all day, contain only pain, but I can't.

NADIA: Why are the words in the vocabulary the gray uses to communicate with us not the same as ours?

PARIS: Maybe because we cannot even access this vocabulary?

MOTHER: I don't know. Not once in my life was I able to translate what the gray was telling me into smiles, happiness, or serenity. Long ago I used to trust in the gray because I was afraid to believe in the white and the black. I am now old and after all these years I can only trust whichever part of my life the gray hates. Now, since I learned how to trust the black and the white, I stopped trusting anything that chooses to live between them.

IRENE: You're right. I have to say that I am often astonished how for someone who has lived his entire life next to the gray, I still don't know what the dam thing is made from, which materials of my life, of myself were used to produce it.

PARIS: How is it possible for us to make the white and black in our lives, the two extremes that define our life, without bothering to find out which materials we used?

IRENE: Are we perhaps making them using ingredients we no longer have the strength to extract on our own from our heart, ingredients we need the help of another heart, one that truly loves us so much that she will bear the pain of taking them in her hands and pulling them out of our own, so we can finally learn what they are?

NADIA: It's incredible how emotionally helpless we are. Why should anyone need someone's help to find out how much compassion she has in her?

ALEXANDER: A happy time of my life, a time that managed to throw off it the disgusting, emotionally heavy gray cape I tried to cover it in, no longer has the ability, like when I was young, to explain to me in just a minute what a sad one has been trying to tell me for hours.

PARIS: How I wish I still had the capacity to resist, to refuse to take hold of the part of myself which my sorrow brings to me at the end of every happy moment in my life.

NADIA: You wouldn't be able to, because you fear it so much that you don't even try to understand it.

ALEXANDER: Let me try to transform myself in my mind, let me transform, even for just a second, into that whisper of mine I admire more than all the screams that are waiting impatiently at the entrance of my heart for me to call them so they can offer me their services.

NADIA: You really like to compromise with any part of your self-confidence you no longer need!

PARIS: Please stop hitting me with those unspoken words that just today decided for the first time after many years to raise their voice from depths of my innards and become cries.

ALEXANDER: Let me borrow for a while the vocabulary my delusions use to convince those defeats of mine which are most proud of their accomplishments to not visit me again today. I need that. Today I need to experience a day that until its end will not ask me to hand over my beliefs as collateral to the part of myself I know less well that any other, so that my self-confidence can get yet another loan she never intends to pay back. I will not be able to bear letting this day drag me by the hand, take me to its end, and drop me off right in front of the entrance midnight uses to let through to tomorrow only those people who, during the day that just ended, couldn't find in their souls enough cowardice to betray their sorrow. And if my poor delusions come at some point to help me experience this, please let them, don't attack them, don't make them feel bad for standing by my side, for supporting me.

IRENE: That doesn't bother me. What bothers me is that after helping you they will push you to climb up the winners podium to award you first prize. I have never met another person in my life who, whatever makes him sad, makes him more beautiful.

ALEXANDER: Why are you so upset by the fact that my tears look better than yours?

IRENE: It's not their look that bothers me, but the fact that they are illiterate. *(Pause)*

PARIS: You know, I am no longer impressed by my tears rarely being able to express what I feel, but I am impressed by their uncanny ability to cry for a different reason than the one I want to cry about!

IRENE: What do you mean?

PARIS: Do you mean that there are often two sorrows living inside you at the same time, the one you show to the world outside and the one you show to your tears, trying to convince them to keep it inside you so you won't be embarrassed?

ALEXANDER: I really wouldn't know how to honestly answer you without insulting my sorrow.

IRENE: There speaks a man who believes there is such a thing as creative sorrow!

ALEXANDER: Why, do you disagree? Don't you believe that a person can create ten joys out of his sorrow? Or, more importantly, a stunning serenity?

IRENE: Not even the tiniest truth was able to fit in between what you told me and what you actually meant to say, no matter how hard she tried. Since we started talking I have seen her come out from time to time and nervously walk back and forth on the edge of your mouth, wanting to jump out without asking your permission.

ALEXANDER: In your case, however, an incredibly full-bodied misery managed to fit in between what you said and what you feel.

IRENE: I think that today we invented a new kind of coldness.

ALEXANDER: How the hell can a word of yours plunge so easily inside me and, grabbing my soul in its hand, start squeezing her with all its strength, till she faints from the pain?

IRENE: I will place my entire body in front of my fist so it won't suddenly decide to attack you.

MOTHER: Come now…Remove at last, from those remote, deep pockets of your souls the mistakes you have been storing all these years as if they are your most valuable possessions. Take them out and leave them on the surface of your life, at the spot where the sun himself is not afraid to wrestle with any darkness, let them free to tap some of the power of the happiness that exists around you, some of the vitality of life's enthusiasm, hoping they will manage to show you, not who they want to hurt, but where they hurt themselves.

IRENE: I no longer fear what I cannot understand, I fear what I am afraid to realize. *(She stops talking and lowers her head as if trying to look inside her)* I have been bleeding this cursed white silence since this morning. The damn thing won't stop. It makes my flesh crawl each time it gets out of my body, and the first thing it does is turn and look into my eyes, and smiling with an enigmatic smile that is more critical than embarrassed, it then forces me to admit, before I even realize it, that out of all of my soul's creations I have selected this white silence to represent me in the world around me.

MOTHER: Every emotion we haven't found a way to feel yet is not necessarily our own creation, our own progeny.

PARIS: It's incredible, isn't it? When you begin to understand what your sorrow is made of, you end up realizing what you are made of too.

NADIA: Listening to you, I feel that today I really want to sit in the front seats of my self-awareness so I can see better. It's already late afternoon and our two bodies are in a hurry to get past the reality our defeatism just left on their surface, so they have time to embrace the longing contained in the sensual pleasure of our common happiness, which wants to learn from scratch how to feel that emotion that she believes our two brains intentionally discarded into our marriage's wake.

PARIS: I feel that we are building a wonderful embrace using the answers we will have once we stop asking ourselves why we love each other.

NADIA: So let our two minds, each one embrace separately our common future so they can try to get a sense of what it wants from each of them to surrender to it.

PARIS: Yes, sure...

NADIA *(Moves towards the fireplace)*: Better yet, let our photos, the ones we have placed over the fireplace to help us remember who we were, provide you with the answer. Set free any emotion of yours that is willing to start translating them for you into something that won't upset your ego. Look at us, hugging each other, arm in arm with the leftovers of all those emotions we felt but never respected, all the questions each one's sorrow wanted to ask the other's joy.

Embracing the questions that always needed to be asked by the future of the ego our relationship has created by combining all the pieces of our two egos it liked best, we have sat in the darkest corner of our life and are waiting to collect the pocket money our normality gave to our passion so that it won't go out in the streets to remind us every so often that there is still so much love, so much soul in our life. Each photo is a portrait of two people that look a lot like us, but their happiness does not look at all like our current happiness. Each one has let his eyes paint on his face a different kind of awkwardness, I can't even see if it's my personal awkwardness, the embarrassment of two people who have in them so many different kinds of sorrow to pick from that, even if they want to, they will rarely happen to feel sad for the same reason.

PARIS: It's so strange, looking at old photographs, to realize that while our physical appearance has changed considerably, our inner world, the one people don't see unless they have to, has changed even more!

ALEXANDER: In every house I visit, I see on the mantelpiece these photos, displaying as advertisements of people who, trying above all to impress their own truth, have put on this bizarre smile, a smile that never understood, the poor thing, why they asked it to be in the picture with them in the first place. It's incredible, as if the only thing they wanted to achieve was to convince themselves, much more than anyone else, that they have to live a life during which they are as happy as they seem in that photo.

MOTHER: It's like those advertising smiles we often use to hide the fact that we don't understand what we are feeling at that moment.

PARIS: I would say that these are the smiles that belong to our misery more than they belong to our happiness, the ones we use to convince her that she is not as unhappy as she thinks.

ALEXANDER: I could never understand why, after showing them photos of the apparently happiest moments of their life, people force their guests to turn around and watch live what remained after the avenging truth of time decided to remove one by one the different special effects with which they tried to cover themselves so that no one could introduce himself to any of them without first introducing himself to his personal fog.

IRENE: I wonder what the future of a relationship feels when it sees the happy photo-ads fill the world all around it, what it feels when it realizes during every minute it has to spend with them what kind of happiness it must compete with daily, what happiness it must surpass to be able to feel it has a chance to survive?

ALEXANDER: It's so sad. We try real hard to put these photos in the most visible part of the house to promote a product that is no longer available...

IRENE: Because it no longer exists…

NADIA: Doesn't it surprise you that, while all the photos are quite colorful, the color that completely dominates is black?

ALEXANDER: Why are you picking on black again? What have you got against black? Don't you understand that it's the only color that can spread its magic body and cover the many parts of its owner which he himself can't stand seeing anymore, let alone display? Why do you refuse to realize that, out of all existing colors, black is the only one that doesn't simply lie when we ask it to, but lies whenever it wants?

MOTHER: And it wants to frequently, very frequently! *(Pause)*

PARIS: That dam black is so useful to me. It always told on my behalf the lies I could not tell myself.

NADIA: I have nothing against black, but I don't owe it anything either. It hasn't done me any favors in my life. On the contrary, it often hurriedly hides from me whichever part of myself I haven't found the courage yet to look in the eyes, but would really like to know what I must do to be able to stand spending a little more time with it. It's that part of myself I would like to get to know better, hoping that someday I will be able to jump up high and fly, even for just a few moments, over my personal abyss and hopefully reach its opposite shoreline, the place where I would like to start my day every morning in the arms of a truth I fell in love with seeing the last moments of my previous sorrow walking disillusioned away from me.

PARIS: You don't mean, I hope, that the truth you fell in love with is the same one you yourself designated later as the last day of your youth?

NADIA: No, I don't.

PARIS: Have we ever tried to answer the questions these photos ask us every day, a few minutes before the sunset begins? Is today perhaps a good day?

NADIA: There is no good day to realize how many fewer colors your own rainbow has compared to other people's.

ALEXANDER: Or to locate the piece of your handshake that is always missing from your hand when you use it to greet someone.

PARIS: You are both right. Today I don't want to force my blood to get out of my body and bring to my mouth the flavor my life has. *(Goes to Nadia and caresses her head)* Let our hearts choose for themselves which shape, out of all the ones the coming dusk is proposing, they feel suits them best.

IRENE *(Turning to Alexander)*: But why haven't we ever managed to both fall in love with the same hope?

ALEXANDER: Because we never found the courage lately to search to find again that word we carefully inserted into our gaze the first time we ever looked at each other.

NADIA: I don't know, but as I get older, I begin to comprehend what an important role the ambition of one's sorrow plays in human relationships.

PARIS: But isn't that the definition of love, when one gives everything to protect the other from his sorrow?

ALEXANDER *(With his head lowered, shaken)*: That must be it.

MOTHER *(To Alexander and Irene)*: While you lived embracing a different winter, each one of you eventually learned to hate the season that follows. You see, you never tried to learn how to trust that day of spring that lives permanently in you. The dreams you used to have together can no longer fit under the overpasses that your minds recently built. They have been waiting for a long time to find you and explain to you those parts of theirs you chose not to understand, so that you won't have to believe them, and by believing them be forced to believe in yourselves, in your ability to realize them. Your marriage has produced on its own an arrogance that is much bigger than the sum of your arrogances put together. In turn, this arrogance has blazed a trail to lead the dreams that your egos have past your own dreams, so that they can start building the future first, before you get a chance to build it yourselves. I wonder, will you ever figure out why you let two vanities as successful as yours load your misery's red handgun with the bullets your own ambition put in your palms just a few bitter words ago?

IRENE *(To Alexander)*: I don't know if you see them, but I can now see the details of our lives nervously trying to find out at which point during our next fight they will be able to buy a draw, any draw. I can clearly see now one's melancholy doing her best to lose the address of the other's happiness as quickly as she can.

ALEXANDER: The zeros we host within us have already started enjoying the company of those triumphs that live in each of our heads, which can no longer remember how to win since they no longer remember what their owners believe in.

IRENE: You mean those zeros that urge us to open them up so we can see which part of ourselves we will find inside them?

MOTHER: More likely those that, because they know what they have in them, beg you to never open them.

IRENE: Can you possibly remember, I wonder, at which point in our relationship we decided for the first time to let these zeros handle all the additions and subtractions in our life that are so important for our future?

ALEXANDER: For the first time? An hour ago, I think.

NADIA: What happens when a person starts to think that his future is more important than his own happiness?

PARIS *(Long silence, lowers his head and, deeply moved, says in a barely audible voice)*: He falls in love with the disaster that is already living in his next triumph. *(Begins to cry)*

MOTHER: But how can you open a gift put together by a courageous silence and your shiest insecurity, a gift that refuses to translate its meaning to any logic that doesn't agree to let it first live inside her for a while before she asks it to explain how it works?

NADIA: The same way you envelop the gaze of the person you love with the first emotion you are unable to feel at that moment and then you let that gaze sit beside you so it can explain what that piece of your heart you could never translate, no matter how hard you tried, into something resembling love, is trying to tell you.

PARIS: Could these moments possibly want to hand over a new vocabulary, so you can learn to read what your disillusioned heart is writing on the outer side of the stone fences

I myself have built in your mind word by word, to protect it from the attacks of my own mistakes? Should you look, perhaps, among these words to find the echo you left in the perpetual safekeeping of your youth, the echo from all the battles you fought in your life without knowing why you had to win them? I have the impression that these are the kind of victories that in the future will not let you live in harmony with them, will always hate you, will always leave you vulnerable to occasional attacks from your self-awareness. You see, these victories knew that, to achieve them, you first had to make your logic seem richer than what she actually was.

NADIA: How?

PARIS: By stealing from the soul of each person you defeated the most sensitive, the most vulnerable, the most defenseless parts, placing them in the most illuminated part of your soul's store display, and dressing them up in your own verbal attire, until they slowly started to look as if they were yours.

NADIA: Perhaps, perhaps…

PARIS: Is this perhaps the reward we had to give our logic in exchange for letting us enjoy what is left of the truth of a relationship once you remove its greatest lie?

NADIA: More likely what we gave her to convince her to leave us alone for a while, to forget us. *(Pause)* By the way, you still haven't told me, can you win over a person without defeating his soul?

PARIS: Out of all the people in the world, you are asking me that?

NADIA *(Begins to speak but stops. Long pause. In the end she says what she meant to say)*: Damn me, I don't know if what you just said has more respect than loathing in it for me.

MOTHER: Don't try to find what you don't want to lose.

NADIA: You mean don't try to lose what we might never find again?

PARIS: I am so glad we both managed to leave the doors to our hearts open during most of this discussion…

NADIA: Not to see which of each other's emotion will manage to enter, but to see if during all this time they will manage not to close on their own. *(Paris tries to talk but Nadia touches his lips with her fingertips to stop him from continuing. She lets go)*

NADIA: When I feel sorry I want to feel sorry just for myself. When I am glad, I want to feel glad for all the people around me. I want to be able to shield you from my own sorrow, to let you live without being swallowed by the huge iron shadow of my melancholy each time the damn thing manages to swallow me. I want to let you enjoy the light of your own life, even if the light of mine has already gotten used to living on its knees, having lost the passion it once had. I feel that whatever glow my life can still bear having comes from deep within me, from that spot where all the wounds I have long been breeding in the part of my soul I always respected less live together.

I have become the toxic echo of my own lies that, living practically isolated in the room of a family that kept the windows to each of their hearts hermetically sealed for years, is having a tough time finding fresh air to breathe. I have been sitting for hours across from the one steep uphill of the part of my life that lives permanently across from me, the one which has painted itself with the brightest rust it found looking through the warehouses of my truth, trying with all the strength I have left in me to find among the leftovers of my honesty the reason why my next joy does not begin where my previous sorrow ends.

MOTHER: Is this, perhaps, the definition of a happy person, one who does not let even the smallest of time intervals of his life get in between the end of his sorrow and the beginning of his next joy?

PARIS: Wait a minute, are you talking about the uphill you don't dare start climbing because you are sure you don't know how to find the way back?

NADIA: Exactly. I have been observing for some time now, at the beginning of this uphill, my honesty, which would do anything to not ever have to climb it, breathing heavily while she ponders the unbearable burden I have forced her to carry on her back on my behalf, namely all my dreams that prefer to remain overweight. You see, I have already demanded that my honesty place my dreams at the peak before I even start climbing. So as I am ascending, I feel an unbearable red silence piecing my ears, while the only sounds that can be heard from the beginning of my optimism to the end of my disillusionment are the unruly echoes of the sound of any spoken truth that can still stand to climb along with me. To make me hurt as much as possible, these sly echoes gather as much speed as they can and slam into the walls of my mind, returning to my ears ten times more repulsive, ten times more harrowing.

MOTHER: You are right, honesties rarely reach the peaks their owners are trying to conquer.

PARIS *(To Nadia)*: How many times did I send words out of my mouth to bring me back from the surface of your eyes victories which did not know to whom they owed the future disasters they were hiding in them... How many times... All these years, not wanting to heal the wounds I inflicted on every passing day myself, I voluntarily sank deeper and deeper into each step my ambiguity took on my behalf, competing with all of you on who will first become the blurred copy of a triumph which, as soon as it won, would refuse to pay the bill for the success itself had ordered. By god, there are dawns when I stand on my melancholy, stomping on her as hard as I can, trying to kill her so that I won't have to see myself once again becoming her ecstatic slave well before midnight.

Holding thirty tiny blue answers in my hand and listening to my compassion tell me two stories at the same time, one for every silence I will use against you in the next few minutes, I finally decide to come and stand right before your truth. I really want to try to grab ahead of her from inside your mouth the first all white word that won't be afraid to abandon your mind and, taking itself a big risk, come to embrace the main fog in my life, and try to caress it to calm it down. This poor word is so scared that, to avoid being seen, it withdrew hours ago, disguising itself as one of those kinds of sorrow I could never recognize without the help of my biggest insecurity.

NADIA: I know that fog, I know it well. It's the thick mist I allowed in the past to sit for countless hours next to me, letting it pressure me into giving it a reason I should not be in love with it. It's the one that never demanded from me to show it where the limits of my sorrow lie, so it won't be forced to learn how to introduce itself to my happiness. Faithfully following me for years, this fog is the only one that was always present at every setback in my life, anxiously running behind me after every grand defeat of mine to cover me with the emotions it thought fit best each time, not me, but the person the people around me wanted to see everytime they looked at me.

MOTHER: Come now... You know that there are no trips to your past that are free...

NADIA: I'm sure that after all these years of daily tossing malfunctioning smiles into the sewer built by hand and given to me by that emotion of mine which has long been residing right across from my happiness, I have taught every next step of my meanness how to be less happy than the one following it without insulting me. Now, not even the infinity that tomorrow keeps at all times inside it can hide in its most secret corners the emotional waste generated by the rage I beget daily, because I can no longer stand feeling ashamed for what I am. And you, all lit up by the enthusiasm your innocence still contains, are standing right in front of me, trying to figure out how much bigger than any of your many kindnesses my meanness is, a meanness which, glaring at you with a look that's even angrier than mine, is trying to convince you to buy me from my biggest lie. Poor man, I did so many bad things to you every time I thought I was doing you good!

MOTHER: I am so glad, because what used to be a launch site of your aggression now dares for the first time to make a u-turn on your life's main boulevard and transform itself into a safe haven.

PARIS: What once was plundered now becomes honestly acquired.

NADIA: What used to be a curse now demands to become the next loving word.

MOTHER: Often in your marriage you ended up abusing the time you were together, and the rape of love cannot turn into romance, but it can be the spot where a truth will grow one day that will want to benefit her owners more than she benefits herself. Maybe the time has come when you realize that every moment of his life man lives in between two walls, the one that is just in front of him which does not let him become a person who is not compatible with his hopes and the wall who follows him just behind which does not let him become a person who is not compatible with his past.

NADIA: Maybe the time has come when we realize what happens to a person when he manages to defeat his own truth.

PARIS: Is it, though, one of those truths that you must conquer in order to be able to live with?

NADIA: I cannot say. As you know, I specialize in a different kind of truth…

THE END

Cover painting
Why would someone want to make his dreams smarter than himself?

Back cover painting
I am sorry you're leaving, but I am glad you are not coming.

www.ingramcontent.com/pod-product-compliance
Lightning Source LLC
Chambersburg PA
CBHW042337150426
43195CB00001B/20